BUILDING TRADITIONAL COUNTRY FURNITURE

BY THE EDITORS OF POPULAR WOODWORKING MAGAZINE

POPULAR WOODWORKING BOOKS

CINCINNATI, OHIO
www.popularwoodworking.com

READ THIS IMPORTANT SAFETY NOTICE

To prevent accidents, keep safety in mind while you work. Use the safety guards installed on power equipment; they are for your protection. When working on power equipment, keep fingers away from saw blades, wear safety goggles to prevent injuries from flying wood chips and sawdust, wear headphones to protect your hearing, and consider installing a dust vacuum to reduce the amount of airborne sawdust in your woodshop. Don't wear loose clothing, such as neckties or shirts with loose sleeves, or jewelry, such as rings, necklaces or bracelets, when working on power equipment. Tie back long hair to prevent it from getting caught in your equipment. People who are sensitive to certain chemicals should check the chemical content of any product before using it. The author and editors who compiled this book have tried to make the contents as accurate and correct as possible. Plans, illustrations, photographs and text have been carefully checked. All instructions, plans and projects should be carefully read, studied and understood before beginning construction. Due to the variability of local conditions, construction materials, skill levels, etc., neither the author nor Popular Woodworking Books assumes any responsibility for any accidents, injuries, damages or other losses incurred resulting from the material presented in this book. Prices listed for supplies were current at the time of publication, and are subject to change. Photocopies or enlargements of any materials in this book are allowed for personal use only.

METRIC CONVERSION CHART

TO CONVERT	TO	MULTIPLY BY
Inches	Centimeters	2.54
Centimeters	Inches	0.4
Feet	Centimeters	30.5
Centimeters	Feet	0.03
Yards	Meters	0.9
Meters	Yards	1.1
Sq. Inches	Sq. Centimeters	6.45
Sq. Centimeters	Sq. Inches	0.16
Sq. Feet	Sq. Meters	0.09
Sq. Meters	Sq. Feet	10.8
Sq. Yards	Sq. Meters	0.8
Sq. Meters	Sq. Yards	1.2
Pounds	Kilograms	0.45
Kilograms	Pounds	2.2
Ounces	Grams	28.4
Grams	Ounces	0.04

Building Traditional Country Furniture. Copyright © 2001 by Popular Woodworking Books. Manufactured in China. All rights reserved. No part of this book may be reproduced in any form or by any electronic or mechanical means including information storage and retrieval systems without permission in writing from the publisher, except by a reviewer, who may quote brief passages in a review. Published by Popular Woodworking Books, an imprint of F&W Publications, Inc., 4700 East Galbraith Road, Cincinnati, Ohio, 45236. First edition.

Visit our Web site at www.popularwoodworking.com for information on more resources for woodworkers.

Other fine Popular Woodworking Books are available from your local bookstore or direct from the publisher.

07   06   05   04   8   7   6

Library of Congress Cataloging-in-Publication Data

Building traditional country furniture / by the editors of Popular Woodworking Books.
    p. cm.
  Includes index.
  ISBN 1-55870-585-6
  1. Furniture making. 2. Country furniture. 3. Shaker furniture. I. Popular Woodworking Books (Firm)
TT194 .B84 2001
684.1′04--dc21   00-050116

Edited by Jennifer Churchill
Editorial assistance by Clara Ellertson
Technical illustrations by Jim Stuard
Designed by Brian Roeth
Production coordinated by Emily Gross
Photography by Al Parrish, Christine Polomsky and Christopher Schwarz
Special thanks to Elaina Stuard for use of the milk-paint game bench, the step stool and one of the Queen Anne side tables. Special thanks to Glen Huey for use of the Shaker hanging cabinet.

PROJECT AUTHORS

Glen Huey, Contributing Editor, *Popular Woodworking* magazine: Table Saw Tenon Jig, Cove Moulding Basics, Martha's Vineyard Cupboard, Shaker Blanket Chest, Six-Legged Huntboard, Pennsylvania Stepback Cupboard, Shaker Hanging Cabinet, Shaker Tailor's Cabinet

Christopher Schwarz, Senior Editor, *Popular Woodworking* magazine: Milk-Paint Game Bench, Military Writing Desk, Burlington Farmer's Desk

Troy Sexton, Contributing Editor, *Popular Woodworking* magazine: $19.99 Dovetail Jig, Four Ways to Build a Tavern Table, Traditional Secretary, Tiger-Maple Medicine Cabinet

Steve Shanesy, Editor & Publisher, *Popular Woodworking* magazine: Shaker Tall Clock, Corner Cupboard

Jim Stack, Editor, Popular Woodworking Books: Tenon Jig Alternative

Jim Stuard, Associate Editor, *Popular Woodworking* magazine: Roadhouse Pipe Box, Butler Tray Table, Queen Anne Side Tables, Shaker Step Stool

David Thiel, Senior Editor, *Popular Woodworking* magazine: Spice Cabinet, Antiqued Tabletop Hutch

Function was foremost in the minds of the early builders of country furniture. Tables had four legs and a top. Cabinets had shelves on which to store things and doors to keep the dust out. Dressers had drawers to hold clothes and other valuables. Keeping it simple meant the furniture was built quickly and did the job.

Although it's American-made, country furniture is overflowing with European influence. The people of many cultural backgrounds that came together in a young, new country implemented styles and techniques from their former homelands, creating a melting-pot flavor in the world of furniture-making.

Woodworkers, by nature, are creative people; it wasn't long before design elements began to appear in these pieces of country furniture being built. A piece of moulding here and an exposed joint there made the pieces more exciting and demonstrated the builders' skills.

This book is a compilation of the more popular country furniture projects we have offered in *Popular Woodworking* magazine. These furniture projects are simple and have a certain basic appeal to a variety of people. Perhaps this is one of the reasons woodworkers love to build them.

Before jumping right in, we will first show you three simple ways to create these projects with a minimum of fuss. The first is a very ingenious method of creating half-blind dovetails with your router and some scrap wood. The second way is an utterly simple jig for making tenons on your table saw. Third, we'll show you that you don't need a shaper to make great-looking cove moulding — just a table saw and a scrap piece of plywood. Then it's on to the building of the furniture!

introduction
acknowledgements

We would like to thank Al Parrish and Christine Polomsky for their wonderful photography of many of the projects. Also, many thanks to all who contributed their building and teaching talents, making these projects possible.

Finally, thanks to the hundreds of now-nameless woodworkers who created and refined these pieces of furniture throughout the decades and made them what they are today.

We hope you enjoy building these timeless pieces of furniture as much as we did.

THE EDITORS OF POPULAR WOODWORKING MAGAZINE

table of *contents*

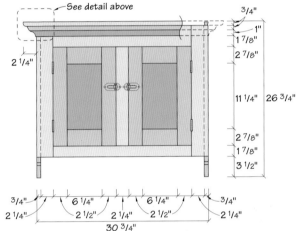

See detail above

3/4"
1"
1 7/8"
2 7/8"
2 1/4"
11 1/4"   26 3/4"
2 7/8"
1 7/8"
3 1/2"

3/4"   6 1/4"   6 1/4"   3/4"
2 1/4"   2 1/2"   2 1/4"   2 1/2"   2 1/4"
30 3/4"

Elevation

You don't have to be a master craftsman or have deep pockets to cut perfect half-blind dovetails.

$19.99 dovetail jig

Seems to me that most people think there are only two ways to cut half-blind dovetails: by hand or with a jig that can cost as much as $300. As someone who makes a lot of custom furniture, I can tell you that neither method has ever worked well for me. Sure, the size and spacing of hand-cut dovetails are easily customized, and it's nice to sometimes work in a quiet shop. But the handwork just takes too long when time is money. Dovetail jigs, on the other hand, are fast. But the size of your drawers is dictated by all but the most expensive jigs on the market.

That's why I've come up with a method that's fast enough to use in a professional furniture shop but allows you to space the tails almost any way you want. The price? Only $11 for a template guide and $8.99 for a carbide-tipped dovetail bit (you'd have to buy both for a dovetail jig, anyway). I've probably made more than 500 drawers using this method, and if you own a router, table saw and band saw, you can make them this way this weekend.

In a nutshell, here's how it works. While you're ripping your drawer pieces to width, rip an extra piece of scrap to use as a template. Use a dado stack in your table saw to cut notches on one end of the template. One notch

for each tail. Clamp the template to the back side of your drawer front. Install the template guide and dovetail bit in your router, set the depth and run the router in and out of the notches. Congratulations. You've just cut the pins.

Now use the pins to lay out the tails on one drawer side. Cut the tails on your band saw. It's simple work. Occasionally you'll then have a little fitting to do, but after a little practice your dovetails will fit snugly the first time.

Get Started

When you're doing this for the first time, keep in mind that all the measurements and settings I'm about to give you apply to drawers with ¾"-thick fronts and ½"-thick sides. I use a $\frac{23}{32}$"-diameter template guide in my router (though $\frac{11}{16}$" or

7

A dado stack in your table saw is all you need to make the template for routing the pins. Don't worry too much about tear-out on the back side of the work. It's just a template.

When you finish making the template, here's what it should look like. For this 3"-wide drawer, I made two notches. Each of the teeth is ¼" wide. You can make the notches almost any width you want. The spacing can be varied by using a smaller template guide in your router.

⅞" will work fine, as well) and a ½"-diameter dovetail bit with sides that slope 14°. See the Supplies box for ordering information.

Begin by making the template. They're really easy to make. So easy, in fact, that I've got dozens of them for almost every size drawer I need. While you're ripping out your drawer parts, rip an extra piece of ⅝"-thick stock for the template. Check the depth of your bushing because the thickness of your template needs to be slightly thicker than the depth of your bushing. For this particular drawer, my sides were 3" wide. Now go to your table saw and set up a dado stack. Don't worry about how wide the dado cut is; the idea here is to get a feel for how this system works. You'll see how to fine-tune the tails after you make a few templates. Set the height of the dado stack to ⅞6". Now set your table saw's fence so there's ¼" of space between the fence and blade. Using your miter gauge and a piece of scrap attached to it, run the

Here you can see how the bushing rides against the template, while the bit cuts the pins. When you cut your pins be sure to stand in front of the work so you can better see what you're doing. I stepped aside for the photo.

supplies

Bushings are available from many catalogs. Woodcraft Supply, (800) 225-1153, carries several universal bushings that fit a wide range of routers. Price of the bushing: $7.50. The locknut costs $3.50.

Carbide-tipped dovetail bits (½" diameter, 14° slope) are available from almost every woodworking catalog and home center. Expect to pay about $8.99 on average, and a little more from specialty bit manufacturers.

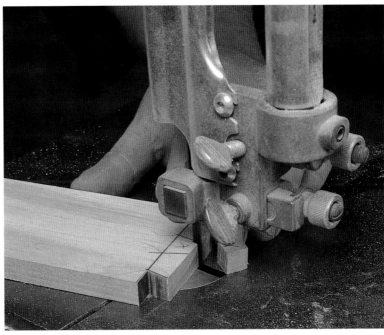

Now lay out the tails by tracing around the inside of your pins. A sharp pencil is key.

Cutting the tails on a band saw is a breeze once you get the hang of it.

template on end as shown in the photo.

Turn the template around and run the other side of the template. Now move the fence away from the blade and remove more material from the template until you have three teeth on the template, each ¼" wide as shown in the photo.

Cut the Pins

Now set up your bench to cut the pins in the drawer front. Put the drawer front facedown on your bench. Line up the template on top of it and clamp the two together to your bench. Install the bushing in your router and then the dovetail bit. Set the bit's height to ¾" (including the bushing on the router's template guide). Different depths will work. I use ¾" because the amount of carbide on my dovetail bit suits that depth perfectly. Cut the pins by running the router in and out of the notches.

Cut the Tails

The hard part is now done. Unclamp your drawer front and place it on top of its mating drawer side as shown in the photo. Using a sharp pencil, trace the outline of the tails onto the drawer side. Cut the tails using your band saw or coping saw. Be sure to cut outside

After a while you'll have enough templates to cut dovetails for almost any drawer.

the lines for a tight-fitting joint. If necessary, pare the tails with a chisel. Then comes the moment of truth.

Let me say that after a couple attempts the truth won't hurt so much, so don't get discouraged. I think you can now see how easy it is to customize the location and size of your tails. Use a smaller-diameter bushing and you can make your tails even closer together. This will require some trial and error

on your part. Basically, the outside teeth will have to be slightly wider than ¼". And if you make different-sized notches in your template, you'll produce drawers that are impossible to make with a $99 dovetail jig. Best of all, you can stop planning your projects around a jig, and you'll be cutting dovetails fast enough to have some hope of finishing your project when you actually thought you would.

9

table saw tenon jig

Several years ago my brother-in-law was thinking about buying a commercial tenoning jig because he was having trouble keeping his work flat against his table saw's small fence while cutting tenon cheeks.

"Don't do that," I told him. "I'll show you how to build a jig from a few pieces of scrap that will do the job just fine." So I built the jig in the photo (at right) and have used it just about every day in my shop to cut tenons on my table saw and sliding dovetails on my router table. The high side and back keep my tenons in position as I cut the cheeks. It's difficult to mess up a tenon with this jig.

When I decided to retire the old jig and build a new one, I thought about adding some fancy features. Then I realized that simple is best, and I stuck with my original design. This jig is built to be used with a commercial Biesemeyer fence. If you don't have a Biesemeyer, you'll have to change the dimensions of the top and side runners, but that's simple to do.

Simplicity Itself

Basically, this jig is two pieces of plywood in an L shape that have a couple pieces of wood screwed to them to allow them to ride the table saw's fence. After settling on the dimensions that are right for your fence, cut all your pieces to size. First clamp the side piece and top runner in position on your fence. Mark where the two pieces

This is the first tenoning jig I built years ago. It's seen a lot of use on my table saw and my router. When I went to build a new jig, I realized that this one served me so well that I didn't need to add any more features to make it more useful.

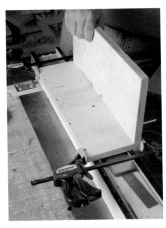

Here's the side piece held in place against the top runner. You want the top runner to be snug against the top of your fence.

The triangular braces keep the side and top runner square and sturdy for years to come.

Take your time fitting the corner brace between the side and back pieces. You want it to hold these pieces at exactly 90°.

Furniture wax works great to keep the runners moving smoothly over your fence. Be sure to reapply wax when the jig starts to get a little stiff after use.

Schedule of Materials: **TABLE SAW TENON JIG**

No.	Ltr.	Item	Dimensions T W L	Material
I	A	Back	$3/4$" x 10" x $15^{1}/4$"	Plywood
I	B	Side	$3/4$" x 10" x 16"	Plywood
I	C	Top runner	$3/4$" x $4^{3}/4$" x 16"	Plywood
I	D	Side runner	$3/4$" x $2^{1}/2$" x 16"	Plywood
2	E	Triangular braces	$3/8$" x 3" x $7^{1}/2$"	Plywood
I	F	Corner brace	$7/8$" x I" x 21"	Hardwood*

* Piece is long; cut to fit.

The curly maple board attached to my miter gauge minimizes tearout when I make the shoulder cuts for my tenons.

After making my cheek cuts (which are shown in the opening photo of the chapter), reset the saw to define the tenon's edge cheeks.

Mortise-and-tenon joints are the staple of my custom woodworking business. I use this jig on every piece of furniture I build. The jig's simplicity and sturdiness have made it one of the workhorses in my shop.

intersect, and screw and glue the two pieces together. Be sure to countersink the screw heads in the side piece. Position the side runner in place under the top runner. You want it to be tight against the fence — but not too tight. Screw it into place.

Now glue and screw the large back piece to the side piece. You want the angle to be 90° between the two pieces, so check your work. Later you'll add a corner brace that will keep this angle fixed at 90°. Attach the two triangular braces to the side and runners. Attach the braces with nails and glue.

Now miter the corner brace to fit. Put an engineer's square between the back and side and adjust the brace until it holds these pieces at exactly 90°. Now nail the brace in place.

Setup and Use

Before you go cutting tenons, wax the areas of the runners that come in contact with your fence. If your jig won't slide, unscrew the side runner and take a light jointer pass on it. When the jig slides smoothly, add some glue to the joint between the side and top runner to make it permanent.

Cutting tenons is now simple. First use your miter gauge and fence to define your shoulders. Then put your jig up on the saw and make your cheek cuts.

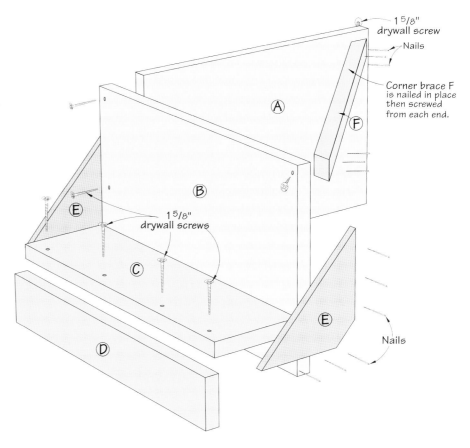

1 5/8"
drywall screw

Nails

Corner brace F is nailed in place then screwed from each end.

Ⓐ

Ⓕ

Ⓑ

Ⓔ

1 5/8"
drywall screws

Ⓒ

Ⓔ

Nails

Ⓓ

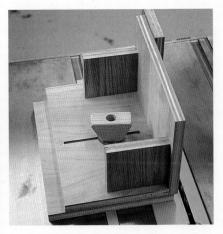

Tenon Jig Alternative

Here's an alternative jig for woodworkers who don't have the table-saw fence style that lets you put Glen's tenon jig to work.

If you don't have a fence that accepts Glen's great tenon jig, here's another version that will work on any table saw. First, cut all parts as shown in the cutting bill. Then, cut a ¹/₄" x 6" slot centered in part B across the width, and screw B and C together, forming a right angle. Attach the two D parts to hold B squarely to C. Drill and countersink a ¹/₄" hole into part A from the bottom so that the hole will line up with the slot in B. Center F on the bottom of A as shown in the drawing and attach it with three ³/₄" screws. Screw part E onto the end of B. (This guide helps the BC assembly to line up and slide squarely on A.) Put the ¹/₄" bolt in place and hold the BCD assembly in place with the fender washer and T-nut knob. (See the detail drawing.) Fit the jig into the miter gauge slot in the table saw top so that F will slide smoothly. Attach upright guide H so it is square to the saw table and you're ready to start cutting tenons.

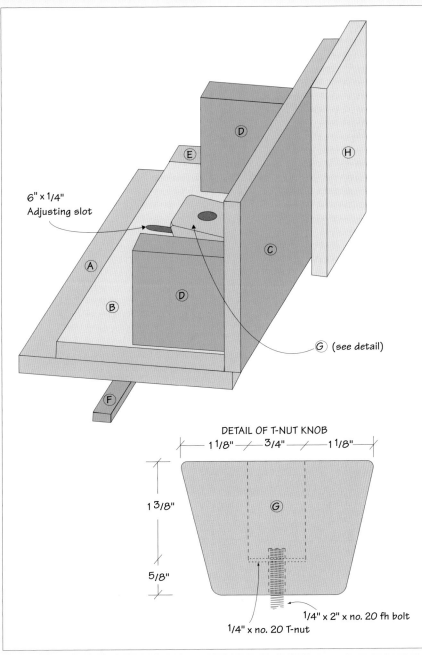

6" x 1/4" Adjusting slot

(A) (B) (C) (D) (E) (F) (H)

G (see detail)

DETAIL OF T-NUT KNOB

1 1/8" — 3/4" — 1 1/8"

1 3/8"

5/8"

(G)

1/4" x 2" x no. 20 fh bolt

1/4" x no. 20 T-nut

Schedule of Materials
TENON JIG ALTERNATIVE

No.	Ltr.	Dimensions T W L
1	A	³/₄" x 9¹/₄" x 11³/₄"
1	B	³/₄" x 7¹/₂" x 11³/₄"
1	C	³/₄" x 7¹/₄" x 11³/₄"
2	D	³/₄" x 4" x 4"
1	E	³/₄" x 1¹/₄" x 8¹/₄"
1	F	³/₈" x ³/₄" x 15"
1	G	1¹/₂" x 2" x 3"
1	H	³/₄" x 4" x 8"

Hardware
1¹/₄" x 2" no. 20 fh bolt
1¹/₄" no. 20 T-nut
1¹/₄" fender washer

You don't need a shaper to make good-looking cove moulding, just a table saw and a scrap of plywood.

cove moulding basics

I use cove moulding on just about every case piece I build. And because I usually work with curly maple (and because I don't want to go broke) I make my own using my table saw and a length of any wood that has a straight edge.

The basic concept is simple. You pass your work over the blade at an angle, using that long straight length of wood as a fence, and nibble away at the wood until you get a nice, concave profile. Then you cut a couple bevels on the edges and sand for a good long while. Let me be the first one to tell you that this procedure is not a science. The setup is a bit tricky, though after a few attempts you can make a piece of cove moulding without a whole lot of trouble. Also, always make a little extra cove moulding for a project in case you botch a miter.

The cove moulding I made for this chapter uses 1" stock that is 4¼" wide. Begin by putting a rip blade in your table saw and cutting a long piece of scrap to use as an auxiliary fence. Why a rip blade? The top of the teeth are flat and will give you a smoother cut. Make a photocopy of the full-size cove pattern on page 17 and glue that to the end of a piece of your stock. Now it's

time to set your auxiliary fence in place.

Where to Put Your Fence

Most books that discuss this procedure advise you to clamp your fence in front of the blade at an angle. This causes the blade to push your work tightly against your fence as you push it through, giving you more control. However, I put my fence behind the blade as you can see in the photos. If you're making cove moulding for the first time, I recommend you put the fence in front of the blade for the first few times. Then after you have some experience, try it my way, which feels more comfortable to me. Rest assured that either way will work fine.

Place your fence across your saw's table and raise the blade to the height of the finished cut, which is a bit shy of ⅝" in this case. Note how many times you turned the wheel of your saw to get there. The trick here is to adjust the fence until the blade lines up, both on the infeed and outfeed sides, with the arc on the pattern you affixed to the wood. Keep adjusting your fence until everything lines up. Then clamp your fence down to your saw. My saw's tableboard is made of plywood, so I merely screw my fence down to my

step 1 *First set your blade to the finished height of the cove cut, using the drawing on the end of a piece of stock.*

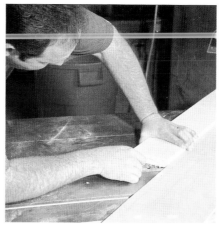

step 2 *Place the auxiliary fence on the top of the saw's table and line up the teeth with the arc drawn on the end of your stock.*

step 3 *Then switch the stock to the infeed side and adjust the angle of the fence to line it up with your arc. Go back to the outfeed side and check it again. When both line up, you're ready to clamp the fence down in position.*

saw. Now put a little wax on your saw's table to make feeding the stock easier.

Cutting the Cove and Bevels

Lower your blade all the way down and then raise it up about ⅛" for your first pass. Run your stock against the fence and raise the blade another ⅛" for the next pass. Keep doing this until you get to your finished height. On the last pass or two, move the stock more slowly (but steadily) over the blade. Also, be sure to keep firm downward pressure on the stock near — but not over — the blade. A slow speed and firm pressure will produce a smoother cut (read: less sanding). Remove the auxiliary fence from your saw and get ready to rip the bevels on the edges.

The bevel on the front of the moulding creates a shadow line between the cove and the case. The angle of your saw blade doesn't have to be exact, but I like to use a 45° angle because that's what I cut on the back side. Use the drawing on the end of your stock to set your table saw's fence. Then rip the two bevels as shown in the photo.

The bevels on the back of the moulding are important because they allow the moulding to fit snugly between the case and a top cap. They need to be at exactly 45°, so cut a test piece or two before cutting the real thing. Again, use the drawing to set your fence and rip the bevels off both edges.

Now take a look at your piece of cove moulding. Do you like the profile? Is it one you think you'll use again? If it is, then cut off a 12"-long chunk of it and put it aside. You'll find it's easier to duplicate a piece of cove moulding if you can use the actual piece of moulding as a template.

Sanding

Cove moulding needs a lot of sanding. In fact, this is the most time-consuming part. One way to speed things up is to replace the standard pad on your random-orbit sander with a very soft one. Most manufacturers make pads with a variety of densities; the only problem is finding the catalog or store that stocks them.

A soft pad follows the curve of the cove moulding better and allows you to remove the saw marks quickly, without flattening the cove.

Before I bought a soft pad for my sander, I sanded cove moulding using a short section of broom handle. Wrap the broom handle with a sanding sponge and then wrap your sandpaper around that.

I wouldn't do all this work if I didn't think the cove moulding made much of a difference, but it does. Cove moulding dresses up a case piece dramatically. In many cases it makes the difference between something plain and something plainly beautiful.

step 4 *I screw my fence in place. If you don't want to poke holes in your tableboard, C-clamps will do just as well.*

step 5 *After years of doing this, I've found that a little furniture wax makes this cut a lot easier.*

step 6 *After the cove cut is made, cut the bevels on the front face of the moulding. Set your saw blade to cut a 45° bevel and rip the edges.*

step 7 *Reset your fence and cut the 45° bevels on the back side of the cove moulding.*

step 9 *The better way to sand cove moulding is to get a softer pad for your ran-dom-orbit sander that will follow the curve of the cove.*

step 8 *If you have to sand your moulding by hand, use a large-diameter dowel or broomstick. Wrap it in a sanding sponge and sandpaper. Then go to work.*

Full-Size Cove Pattern

Though I swiped about 50 percent of the look of this piece from an antique, the joinery is 100 percent traditional.

MARTHA'S
VINEYARD CUPBOARD

A few summers ago my wife and I were traveling through Martha's Vineyard on vacation when we stopped at a small antiques store. On one wall was a simple hanging cupboard with two flat panel doors. Its simplicity and convenience caught my eye, and I had never seen one quite like it before. Rather than buying the piece, I took a photo and thanked the storekeeper for her time. Once home I spent some time rethinking the cupboard and redesigned it to add some details, including the beading on the door edges and the back slats. The original had been made of pine, but I opted for a more dramatic bird's-eye maple for the exterior with painted poplar inside.

Here's how the cupboard goes together: Sliding dovetails hold the top to the two sides. The center shelf and bottom rest in dadoes cut in the sides. To strengthen the cabinet, I use traditional square pegs to attach the shelf, bottom, face frame and doors. And I've got a great trick to get the pegs to fit easily. See the sidebar "Square Pegs, Round Holes" to learn how.

Construction begins by planing the wood to proper thickness, then cutting the top, sides, bottom and shelf to size. Next, using the diagram, mark the dado locations on the sides and cut the ½"-deep dadoes. Cut ¾"-wide by ⅜"-thick

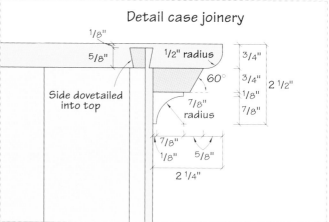

Schedule of Materials: MARTHA'S VINEYARD CUPBOARD

No.	Item	Dimensions T W L	Material
1	Top	3/4" x 10 1/2" x 35 1/4"	P
2	Sides	3/4" x 7" x 26 5/8"	P
2	Shelves	3/4" x 6 1/4" x 30 1/4"	S
2	Face frame stiles	3/4" x 3" x 22 1/2"	P
1	Frame lower rail	3/4" x 1 7/8" x 26 3/4"	P
1	Frame top rail	3/4" x 3 5/8" x 26 3/4"	P
1	Frame center stile	3/4" x 2 1/4" x 19"	P
4	Door rails	3/4" x 2 7/8" x 9"	P
4	Door stiles	3/4" x 2 1/2" x 17"	P
2	Door panels	1/2" x 6 7/8" x 11 7/8"	P
1	Hanging strip	3/4" x 1 3/4" x 29 1/4"	S
7	Beaded back boards	3/4" x 4 13/16" x 22 1/2"	S
4 1/2	Linear feet of 1" x 1" cove moulding		
4 1/2	Linear feet of 3/4" x 1 5/8" intermediate moulding		

P = Primary wood: Bird's eye maple
S = Secondary wood: Poplar

Detail case joinery

1/8"

5/8"

Side dovetailed into top

1/2" radius

60°

7/8" radius

3/4"

3/4"

1/8"

7/8"

2 1/2"

7/8"

1/8"

5/8"

2 1/4"

Cut the sliding dovetail on the sides using a homemade jig. Cut the female part first, then cut the male part as shown here.

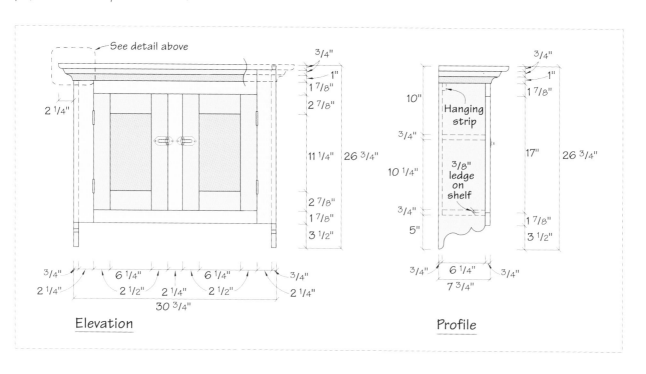

Elevation

Profile

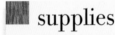

Here are the doors, before assembly and after. Notice the haunched tenon on the rails to hide the panel groove.

supplies

Horton Brasses, Inc.
(800) 754-9127
www.horton-brasses.com
2 - Door catches #SL-3,
    $11.00 each
2 - Pair - hinges #DH-2-125,
    $4.50 a pair

After you've dry fit the case, disassemble the case, add the glue in the dadoes and clamp it up. Drill the clearance holes for the square pegs and knock the pegs home.

rabbets on the sides to hold the back. The scrollwork pattern for the bottom edge of the sides is available at our Web site at: www.popwood.com/fixes/scroll.htm

The next step is to plow the dovetail slot in the top piece, then form the ½"-long sliding dovetail pin on the top end of the sides. Again, find the location for milling the top on the diagrams. A router table works well for both steps, running the top flat on the table, and the sides on end against a fence. Now cut a ½" roundover on the front and sides of the top.

With all the pieces milled, assemble the carcass. Dry fit the pieces and clamp them in place. Unclamp the piece, add glue and reassemble the carcass. Clamp it up, then drill ¼" clearance holes for the pegs through the sides and into the shelf and bottom and drive the 1½"-long square pegs into the ¼" holes.

The face frame uses mortise-and-tenon joinery for strength. Once you've cut the 1"-long tenons and the mortises, dry fit the face frame. Locate and cut the recesses for the hinges on the stiles. Glue and clamp up the face

frame. When dry, drill for pinning the mortise and tenon with square pegs. Then fit the frame to the front of the carcass, apply glue and peg the frame in place.

The back pieces use a ⁵⁄₁₆" × ⅜" mating rabbet (or shiplapped joint) to allow movement in the pieces while still maintaining a gapless back. The back pieces rest in a rabbet cut in the sides, against the shelves and the hanging strip. The hanging strip is nailed between the sides and flush against the top, ¾" in from the back edge. Once the back pieces are cut to size, run the

Square Pegs, Round Holes

I'm sure you know the adage about how you can't fit a square peg into a round hole. But I'm here to tell you that in woodworking you can fit a square peg in a round hole using a pencil sharpener. I start with $1/4$" x $1/4$" square pegs and then sharpen them in the pencil sharpener. Then I add a little glue and pound them in place in the $1/4$" clearance holes I've drilled in the project. The round part slips in easily, and then the square part cuts into the round edges of the hole — creating the illusion of a square hole. Some people add the square pegs after finish sanding, then sand them so they're just a little proud of the surface. It's a traditional method. Plus, if you sand the pegs flush, you'll sometimes start to reveal some of the round shape of the hole.

mating rabbets on the edges (except for the two outside pieces). As a nice detail I used a moulding cutterhead in my table saw to run a single bead on the inside edge of each piece. Test the fit of the back pieces, but leave them unattached at this time to make finishing easier.

The next step is to make the doors. Like the face frame, they are assembled using mortise-and-tenon joinery, with the rails captured between the stiles. The door tenons are 1⅛" long. Cut a ¼" × ⅜"-deep groove in the center, inside edge of each door piece to hold the panel, which has a ¼" × ⅜"-long rabbet on all four sides to form a tongue. Don't forget to cut a bead on the outside edge of each stile.

Assemble the doors using glue in the mortises, but keep the glue out of the panel grooves to allow the panel to float in the door frame. Again, drill the mortise-and-tenon joints and add square pegs for strength. After the glue is dry, locate and recess the hinge locations, then fit the doors, allowing space for the hinges.

The last construction detail is to add the intermediate and cove moulding to the underside of the top to finish off the upper section of the cabinet. The diagram shows the orientation of the pieces. Miter the moulding to fit, then

The back is shiplapped and nailed in place. Because the back is the last thing to go in, I paint the back pieces while finishing the rest of the cupboard. Then, when everything is dry, nail the back in place to the hanging strip and shelves.

nail it in place.

Paint the interior of the cabinet. The exterior is finished with a homemade finish of equal parts boiled linseed oil, varnish and turpentine. I follow that up with a coat of wax. After the finish has dried, attach the hardware and doors and add wall hangers for mounting the cabinet.

SPICE
CABINET

Though members of your family aren't likely to store spices in a cabinet like this, you can bet that it will be an oft-requested item for you to build. So you might want to think about making more than one when you begin.

Cut the sides and ends to size, then cut ½" finger joints on the ends of each piece. Next cut ¼" × ½"-wide dadoes on the sides and ends as located on the diagrams. Cut a ¼" × ½"-wide rabbet on the back edge of each side for the back.

Next, cut the three dividers to size, and with the case dry-clamped together, check the dimensions of the dividers against your case. Trim them to fit, then cut ½"-wide bridle joints to fit the dividers together. Glue up the case, holding the dividers' front edges flush to the case front. When dry, sand the

joints flush to the outside surfaces.

Cut the hanger to shape from the diagrams, then glue and nail the hanger in place at the back of the cabinet. Now cut the back to size and nail it in place.

Next cut the drawer box pieces to size. Then cut ⅛" × ¼"-wide rabbets on the ends of the sides and cut ⅛" × ¼"-deep dadoes for the bottoms on the ends and sides, starting ⅛" up from the bottom edge. To assemble, glue and nail the drawer boxes together.

Cut the drawer fronts to size, then make the knobs. Cut a ⅜" × 1" × 8" strip

of cherry, beveling the sides at a 25° angle. Then cut the knobs off at 1" intervals, again beveling the sides at 25°. Either use a band saw to cut the knobs to shape, or sand them to shape after separating. Attach the knobs to the drawer fronts with no. 4 flathead screws and glue. Glue the fronts to the drawer boxes.

Before finishing the piece, distress the cabinet with keys, screwdrivers and a hammer. I applied brown mahogany gel stain; when the stain was dry, I then applied a coat of wax.

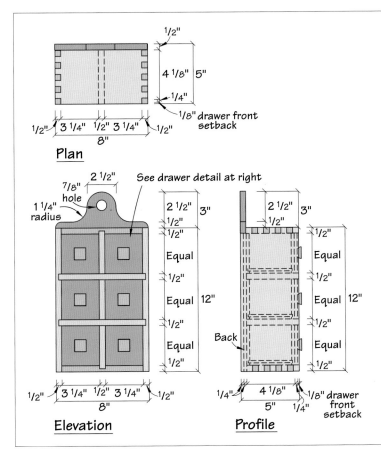

Plan

Elevation

Profile

Schedule of Materials: SPICE CABINET

No.	Item	Dimensions T W L	Material
2	Sides	½" × 5" × 12"	Cherry
1	Bottom	½" × 5" × 8"	Cherry
1	Top	½" × 4⁹⁄₁₆" × 8"	Cherry
1	Center	½" × 4½" × 11½"	Cherry
2	Dividers	½" × 4½" × 7½"	Cherry
1	Hanger	½" × 8" × 3½ "	Cherry
1	Back	¼" × 7½" × 11"	Plywood
6	Drawer fronts	¼" × 3¼" × 3⁵⁄₁₆"	Cherry
12	Drawer sides	¼" × 3³⁄₁₆" × 4⅛"	Plywood
12	Drawer ends	¼" × 3³⁄₁₆" × 3"	Plywood
6	Drawer bottoms	¼" × 2¹⁵⁄₁₆" × 3⅞"	Plywood
6	Drawer knobs	⅜" × 1" × 1"	Cherry

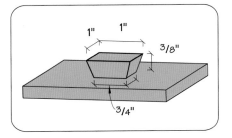

Detail of drawer front

Brother Benjamin Youngs' clock is an exquisite example of how a simple Shaker design can carry across the ages, and still have a foot firmly planted in two centuries.

SHAKER
TALL CLOCK

Here are my great-grandfather's drawing tools.

You'd never guess what the most inspiring aspect of building this clock was. Not the awesome curly maple or rich-looking finish, but something altogether plain — the clock's paper face.

Nice, but what's so special about it, you ask? It was hand-drawn and -lettered using 100-year-old drawing instruments passed down from my great-grandfather, a draftsman, who laid out track beds for the railroads. The set, made in Manchester, England, by A.G. Thornton & Co. and lovingly stored in a velvet-and-satin-lined walnut box, contains calipers, two delicately turned ivory-handled inkers and finely tooled and incredibly machined compasses.

Horology 101

I didn't know what *horology* meant when I received the big box full of clock parts for this project. Fortunately, I had a dictionary, so I quickly learned it means "the art of making time pieces." Too bad there wasn't a reference for identifying and assembling the clock parts. I'm still a long way from being an expert, but for this project at least, I think I can talk you through it.

The *works* are the gears and movements that are sandwiched between a front and back plate. The works for this project are made by Hermle, are weight-driven, require resetting the chains every eight days, strike a bell once on the half hour and ring the hour with the number of rings for the hour struck.

The works have the stem for the hands facing front, of course, and the pendulum faces rear. The pendulum attaches to the works with a narrow, metal part called a leader. The works require two weights suspended on two chains. One weight drives the timekeeping job of the works, the other provides the energy to make the chimes work. The weights use equal lengths of chain and so are reset at the same time.

When facing the works, the chains go over the sprockets with the weights on the outside of each sprocket. When you set the chains on the sprockets, make sure they are not twisted and are seated properly. The weights are attached to the chains with an S-hook.

Each lead weight goes inside a brass tube called a shell. Each tube has two end caps with holes where a rod with threaded ends goes through, which keeps the whole thing together, with a nut on the bottom and hook on the top.

The hands of the clock fit on the stem, which consists of two parts, one inside the other. The hour hand goes on first and sleeves over the outside part of the stem. Press the hand on in the appropriate direction of the given hour. The minute hand, on the other hand (sorry!), has a square bushing and sleeves onto the inner part of the stem. It must be adjusted by turning the bushing that's pressed into the hand. A decorative brass nut holds the minute hand in place.

The pendulum helps regulate the speed of the clock. If it's running fast, you adjust the brass-colored circle down, making the travel of the swing longer. Moving it up shortens the travel, making the clock faster if it's running slow.

The beat of the clock — that's the rhythm of the ticktock sound — is also important. Like your heart, it wants to be regular. Tap your finger to each ticktock sound. The time between taps should be equal. Adjust the beat by moving the escapement ever so slightly. The escapement is the C-shaped metal part in the center upper back of the works. It regulates the gear that's connected by a rod to the top of the leader from which the pendulum hangs.

The works are attached to the top of the box on which it mounts using two long, thin machine screws. They thread into tapped holes in the lower bars, which hold the front and back metal plates of the works together. The works are mounted to a plywood box that rests on the lower case.

Gluing up the top case was made a lot easier by these 90° clamps. Getting things square was a real snap.

After experimenting with these special tools I was ready to put pen to parchment. As I did so, I was amazed with the tool's ability to guide the drawing tip, rendering the precise lines. In making my clock face I imagined for a brief moment looking over my great-grandfather's shoulder as he sat at his drawing board.

Using this old way of drawing was infinitely simpler to figure out than assembling the various parts that made up the clock's works. Most parts were obvious as to their function: the works, pendulum, weights, chain, etc. But how they mounted, attached or were oriented to each other was a complete mystery. They arrived in a kit without the first hint of instruction, and left me scratching my head. Thank goodness building the clock's case was easier than figuring out the works.

Easier, because I had the help of three books referencing this famous clock made by Brother Benjamin, so determining overall dimensions was relatively easy, save for the fact none of them agreed exactly.

The original Shaker clock was built from poplar, but I had just enough curly maple to do the job. One board was even wide enough to make the 12"-wide front, which is where I began construction. To keep the look of a

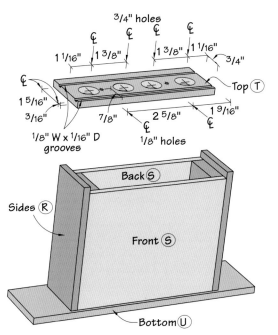

Detail of hole locations in riser box

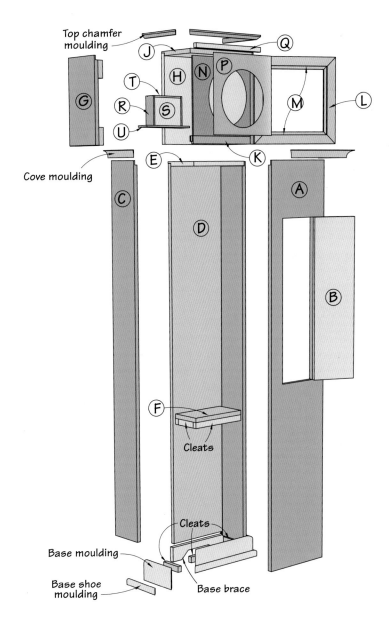

Schedule of Materials: **SHAKER TALL CLOCK**

Lower Case

No.	Ltr.	Item	Dimensions TWL	Material
1	A	Front	$3/4$" x 12" x 65"	P
1	B	Door	$3/4$" x $6^7/8$" x $25^7/8$"	P
2	C	Sides	$3/4$" x $6^1/4$" x 65"	P
1	D	Back	$3/4$" x $11^1/2$" x $64^3/4$"	PL
1	E	Top	$3/4$" x $6^3/4$" x $11^1/2$"	PL
1	F	Bottom	$3/4$" x $5^1/2$" x $11^1/2$"	PL

Upper Case

No.	Ltr.	Item	Dimensions TWL	Material
2	G	Sides	$3/4$" x $7^1/2$" x 15"	P
1	H	Back	$3/4$" x 14" x $14^3/4$"	P
1	J	Top	$3/4$" x $7^1/2$" x 14"	PL
1	K	Front rail	$3/8$" x $1^1/4$" x $13^3/4$"	P
2	L	Dr stiles	$3/4$" x 2" x $14^3/16$"	P
2	M	Dr rails	$3/4$" x 2" x $14^9/16$"	P
1	N	Face pnl	$1/4$" x 13" x $12^{13}/16$"	H
1	P	Face cvr	13" x $12^{13}/16$"	C
1	Q	Buildup	$3/4$" x $3/4$" x $14^1/2$"	P

Clockworks Stand

No.	Ltr.	Item	Dimensions TWL	Material
2	R	Sides	$3/4$" x 2" x $4^3/16$"	S
2	S	Frnt/bk	$1/4$" x $4^7/16$" x $5^1/2$"	PL
1	T	Top	$1/4$" x 2" x $5^1/2$"	PL
1	U	Bottom	$1/4$" x $2^3/8$" x 9"	PL

Mouldings

Top chamfer 36" of $3/4$" sq.
Cove 36" of $2^1/8$" sq.
Base 36" of $3/4$" x $3^1/2$"
Base shoe $1/2$" x 1"

P = Primary wood: Maple • PL = Plywood • S = Secondary wood: Poplar • H = Hardboard • C = Copper

Here are the bonnet, glazing compound, face, copper surround and cleats for attachment.

Here is the 10-minute homemade cockbeading tool in use.

single-board front, cut the board to length, then rip from each edge the "stiles" at the door opening. Cut out the door opening 30" up from the bottom, then 9" from the top. When done, mark the orientation of the pieces. Now glue the front together, less the opening for the door.

Next, cut a ½" × ⅜" rabbet along the inside back edge and top edge of the two side pieces. Mill the same rabbet on the top of the front piece, and on the back edge of the top, as well. While working on the top, also make the cutout to accommodate the swinging pendulum and the hanging chains from the works (see diagram). The front and sides are then glued up using a simple butt joint to take advantage of the long-grain to long-grain connection, while the top is glued and nailed in place. Before screwing in the back, fasten cleats to the front and sides to be used later to attach the bottom panel.

When the case is complete, make the two-part base using a ½"-radius profile bit for the wider piece and ¼" for the smaller base shoe. Miter the front corners and cut a rabbet on the other end for the base back. The front and sides of the base sleeve over the lower

case about 1" and are fastened from the inside of the case.

The upper case that shrouds the clock's works uses the same joints for the back and top as in the lower case. A ⅞"-thick rail is haunch tenoned and mortised into the sides at the bottom of the front to hold the sides square and in place. (See page 38 for an explanation of haunched tenons.) When it's glued up and still in the clamps, pin the tenons using ⅛" dowel stock. After the upper case is assembled, add a filler strip to the front upper edge that's as long as the front is wide and ⅞" square.

Here you can see the cutouts to accommodate the swinging pendulum and the hanging chains from the works.

This buildup accommodates the thickness of the door so that the top chamfered moulding is correctly positioned.

The upper door has a cockbead detail on its outside edge. To create the detail, take 10 minutes to make a simple scratch stock using a flathead screw. Simply insert the screw in the end of a block that fits comfortably in your hand. Let the head project out about ¼". With a hacksaw, cut the projecting screw head in half from top to bottom. Dress the cutting edge (the face) with a file, and use a small triangular file to relieve the back.

Cut the cockbead on the milled stock for the door frame, then cut a ½"-square rabbet on the back inside edge of the stock to let in the glass. Now cut the parts to length and glue up.

Now, make the last mouldings you'll need. The chamfer at the top is easy. Run it, miter the corners and judiciously nail it in place. I used only a dab of polyurethane glue at the center of the moulding because its grain runs contrary to that of the sides.

The cove moulding is more difficult to produce and is made from a triangular-shaped length of wood using the table saw. Clamp an auxiliary fence at a severe, oblique angle to the blade, then run the part with the blade just above the table, raising it slightly after each pass. Thank goodness only about three linear feet are required, because this method

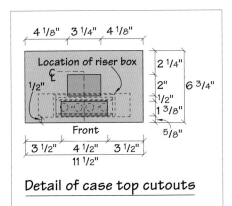

4 1/8" 3 1/4" 4 1/8"

Location of riser box
℄
1/2"

2 1/4"
2"   6 3/4"
1/2"
1 3/8"

Front
5/8"

3 1/2" 4 1/2" 3 1/2"
11 1/2"

Detail of case top cutouts

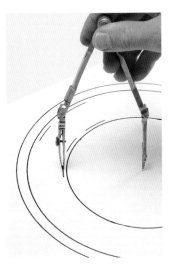

*It's simple work to ink the lines for the paper face. After you make the three circles, use a compass to ink the top and bottom of the roman numerals **(far left)**. Then ink the straight lines to fill in the numerals. It's not calligraphy, so you don't have to worry about curving lines **(left)**.*

requires a lot of sanding to remove the mill marks from the blade. When finished sanding, cut the miters and attach it just like the chamfer moulding.

You may be wondering how the top case attaches to the lower. It doesn't. It simply rests on top and lifts off to access the works (after removing the hands).

I used the clock face supplied in the clockworks package as a guide to lay out my paper face. Construction need not change if you use the painted aluminum face in the kit. In either case, fix the clock face to ¼" tempered hardboard using spray adhesive. Then drill a ⁵⁄₁₆" hole in the center of the face.

I'm sure Brother Youngs didn't use copper sheet metal to surround the face outside the clock face proper, but I did. I made the round cutout using a router mounted on a circle-cutting jig. It's a very simple process. When done, I used a random-orbit sander and 220-grit paper to put a satinlike sheen on the copper, followed by a coat of shellac to retard tarnishing. The hardboard and copper are mounted inside the upper case on cleats positioned to coincide with the mounting location of the works (see diagram).

The last bit of building is the small box on which the works sit. Its height is especially critical because that determines the height at which the stem protrudes through the hole in the face. Make the box using ¾" solid poplar sides and ¼" Baltic birch top and bottom. Note that the bottom is wider and longer than the top. Use the extra length to screw it down. Follow the diagram to position the holes in the top of the box where the chains run through.

Before the upper door can be hung, you must install the glass. I used glass from stock I salvaged from old houses. This old material has imperfections in the thickness that cause ever-so-slight distortions and add to the authentic look of the piece. Regardless of the glass you use, install it using glazing points and glazing compound.

Now the upper door is ready to hang. The hinges in the clock kit don't require mortising, so attach them directly. The lower door is the same. However, before hanging the door, run a ¼"-radius profile on the outside edges. Then attach the hinges to allow it to set ¼" proud of the case.

It goes without saying that I was just itching to set up the works and check everything out. It's a good idea to do this before sanding and finishing anyway. Set it up and let it run overnight.

Use a random-orbit sander to thoroughly sand all the surfaces, starting with 100 grit and progressing up to 180. Break all the edges by hand with 120 grit. After removing the dust, color the wood using J.E. Moser's Golden Amber Maple water-based aniline dye (see the Supplies box for ordering in-

formation). Because the water raises the grain, very carefully and lightly hand-sand the flat surfaces with 360-grit paper. Be extremely cautious near edges. Don't sand through the color. Dust again, then apply a light coat of boiled linseed oil. As a penetrating finish, the boiled linseed oil plays an important role in making the curly figure on the wood pop. When done, rub down with a clean rag to remove any excess oil. Wait 24 hours to allow the oil to dry, then brush on four coats of amber shellac in a two-pound cut. Lightly sand between coats to produce a smooth finish.

The unusual experiences of learning how to set up a mechanical-works clock and creating the clock face from my heirloom drawing set added a new dimension to the satisfaction I always find at the conclusion of a project. I felt in touch with a distant branch of my family tree, rather than merely reproducing an artifact from the past. Some day, should my tall clock find its way into one of my children's homes, I hope my name, scrawled on the clock face, will impart a similar sentiment.

Get ready for the chilly winter nights with this faithful reproduction of a classic from Canaan, New York.

SHAKER
BLANKET CHEST

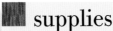 **supplies**

Horton Brasses, Inc.
(800) 754-9127
www.horton-brasses.com
I Pair, 8" strap hinges, #HF-9

Ball and Ball
(800) 275-3711
www.ballandball-us.com
I Box lock, #TJI-062

Woodworker's Supply
(800) 645-9292
J.E. Moser's Early American
Cherry aniline dye, #W1430

I was flipping through a copy of *The Magazine Antiques* one afternoon when I noticed an attractive blanket chest in an advertisement for an antiques dealer in New York. The ad said the Shaker chest was from the John Roberts house in Canaan, New York, and had been built in 1850. All I knew was I wanted to build one. With a bit of research on traditional Shaker joinery, it was off to the shop.

The chest is built exactly as Shakers did in the 19th century — with the notable exceptions of biscuits to attach the feet, aliphatic resin glue and a few power tools that would have shocked and excited the brethren. You'll probably need to glue up a few boards to create panels wide enough for the sides, front and top, unless you have access to some lumber in legendary 19th-century widths. Prepare the panels for the sides, front, upper back and top. You might also have to glue up panels for the larger drawer pieces.

Start with the two sides. Determine the best face and mark it for the out-

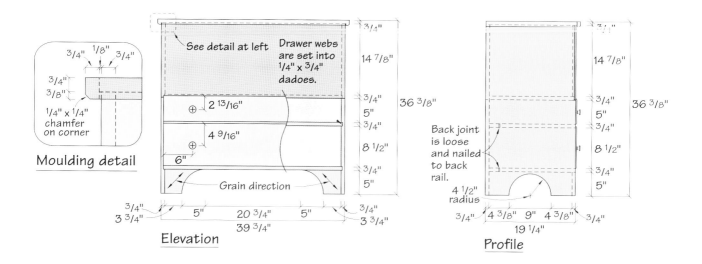

Moulding detail

3/4" · 1/8" · 3/4"

3/4"

3/8"

1/4" x 1/4" chamfer on corner

See detail at left · Drawer webs are set into 1/4" x 3/4" dadoes.

3/4"

14 7/8"

2 13/16"

4 9/16"

6"

Grain direction

3/4"

3/4"

5"

3/4"

8 1/2"

3/4"

5"

36 3/8"

3/4" · 5" · 20 3/4" · 5" · 3/4"

3 3/4" · 3 3/4"

39 3/4"

Elevation

3/4"

14 7/8"

Back joint is loose and nailed to back rail.

4 1/2" radius

3/4"

5"

3/4"

8 1/2"

3/4"

5"

36 3/8"

3/4" · 4 3/8" · 9" · 4 3/8" · 3/4"

19 1/4"

Profile

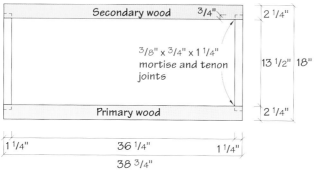

Secondary wood · 3/4"

3/8" x 3/4" x 1 1/4" mortise and tenon joints

Primary wood

2 1/4"

13 1/2" · 18"

2 1/4"

1 1/4" · 36 1/4" · 1 1/4"

38 3/4"

Plan of drawer web frame

step 1 *The front feet are different from the back feet and are cut to allow the grain to run diagonally from the corner of the base area. In addition, the front feet are radius cut on the inside. Attach the feet first, then cut the radius to shape to ease glue-up.*

side, then mark the location of the three dadoes for the bottom and the two drawer divider webs as shown in the diagram. The dadoes are ¾" wide and ¼" deep and run the entire width of the sides. With the dadoes cut, next turn to the ¾" × ¾"-deep rabbet on the back edge of each side. This rabbet should stop 5" up from the bottom of each side to leave a solid gluing surface for the rear feet.

Notch the sides on the front edge ¾" deep to allow the front to overlap the sides. This notch will match the front width. Finally, cut a half-circle on each side to form the feet of the base. Use a 4½" radius to mark the half-circle, then cut it out with a jigsaw.

With the sides complete, turn to the front piece and cut a ¾" × ¾" rabbet on each end and the bottom. The rabbets allow the front to fit into the notches on the front edge of each side, and they also allow the bottom to fit snugly into the front. The last step before assembling the case is to prepare the drawer web frames. The drawer runners have a ¾"-long tenon cut on either end that fits into matching mortises cut in the front and rear dividers. Glue the front mortise-and-tenon joint but leave the back one loose to allow the frame to expand and contract.

Attach the front and rear feet to the bottom divider frame and case sides with biscuits. The Shakers might have used only glue at this joint, but because we have the technology, cut biscuit

Schedule of Materials: **SHAKER BLANKET CHEST**

No.	Item	Dimensions T W L	Material
2	Sides	$\frac{3}{4}$" x 19$\frac{1}{4}$" x 35$\frac{5}{8}$"	P
I	Front	$\frac{3}{4}$" x 16" x 39$\frac{3}{4}$"	P
I	Back	$\frac{3}{4}$" x 16" x 39$\frac{1}{8}$"	P
I	Bottom	$\frac{3}{4}$" x 18$\frac{1}{8}$" x 38$\frac{3}{4}$"	S
I	Top	$\frac{3}{4}$" x 19$\frac{3}{8}$" x 40"	P
4	Drawer dividers	$\frac{3}{4}$" x 2$\frac{1}{4}$" x 38$\frac{3}{4}$"	P/S
4	Drawer runners*	$\frac{3}{4}$" x 1$\frac{1}{4}$" x 15$\frac{3}{8}$"	S
2	Rear feet	$\frac{3}{4}$" x 5" x 5"	S
2	Front feet	$\frac{3}{4}$" x 6$\frac{1}{2}$" x 14$\frac{1}{2}$"	P
2	Buildup blocks	$\frac{3}{4}$" x 2$\frac{1}{2}$" x 4"	P
I	Small drawer front †	$\frac{13}{16}$" x 5$\frac{5}{16}$" x 38$\frac{7}{8}$"	P
I	Large drawer front †	$\frac{13}{16}$" x 8$\frac{13}{16}$" x 38$\frac{7}{8}$"	P
I	Small drawer back	$\frac{9}{16}$" x 4$\frac{7}{8}$" x 38$\frac{1}{4}$"	S
I	Large drawer back	$\frac{9}{16}$" x 8$\frac{3}{8}$" x 38$\frac{1}{4}$"	S
2	Small drawer sides	$\frac{9}{16}$" x 4$\frac{7}{8}$" x 17"	S
2	Large drawer sides	$\frac{9}{16}$" x 8$\frac{3}{8}$" x 17"	S
2	Drawer bottoms	$\frac{5}{8}$" x 17$\frac{1}{4}$" x 37$\frac{1}{2}$"	S
	Backboards ‡	$\frac{5}{8}$" x 15" x 39$\frac{1}{8}$"	S

6 linear feet of $\frac{5}{8}$" x 1$\frac{1}{16}$" bevel-edged top moulding
4 1$\frac{1}{2}$"-diameter wooden knobs

* $\frac{3}{4}$" tenon on both ends
† $\frac{5}{16}$" lip side and top, $\frac{1}{8}$" bottom
‡ Size given is size of complete, half-lapped back
P = Primary wood: Maple • S = Secondary wood: Poplar

step 2 *With the case glued up and the upper back in place, the loose lower back pieces are ready to be nailed in place. The half-lap design provides a closed back, but allows the wood to expand and contract with the wood movement.*

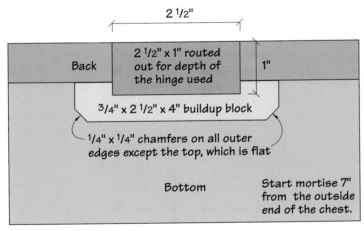

2 1/2"

Back

2 1/2" x 1" routed out for depth of the hinge used

1"

3/4" x 2 1/2" x 4" buildup block

1/4" x 1/4" chamfers on all outer edges except the top, which is flat

Bottom

Start mortise 7" from the outside end of the chest.

Plan detail of hinge buildup

slots for all the feet.

The case is now ready to assemble, but I'd recommend first taking a couple of minutes to finish sand the interior of the blanket chest area. It's tough to get into those corners once the chest is together. Little glue should be used to assemble the chest. A dot of glue at the center of the bottom dado and a dot at the ends of the web frame dadoes is sufficient. Nail the web frames in place

with a single nail through the sides and into the end of the dividers. Nail the front and back pieces in place without glue because the joints are long-grain to short-grain joints.

Complete the case assembly by gluing the front and rear feet in place. When the glue is dry, cut the radius on the front feet to match the curve on the sides and sand your handiwork. Finally, nail the shiplapped back pieces in

place using nickels as spacers.

Next prepare the chest for the top. The chest top needs a stout hinge that requires more than the ¾" back to support it. To accomplish this, glue and nail buildup blocks to the chest back. Once the blocks are fixed in place, use your router and a straight bit to cut a mortise in the back and block for the hinge leaf.

Now prepare the moulding that's attached to the front edge and sides of the top. The moulding is more than decorative; it also forms a dust seal across the lid. First bevel the moulding on the bottom edge to soften the corner, miter the pieces, and then nail it flush to the top edge.

Position the top on the chest with the back edges flush. Mark the hinge location on the top, then attach the hinges.

Now it's time to work on the drawers. The drawers are assembled using rabbeted half-blind dovetails at the front and through-dovetails at the rear. First rabbet the drawer fronts to form a $\frac{5}{16}$" lip on the top and sides, and an $\frac{1}{8}$"

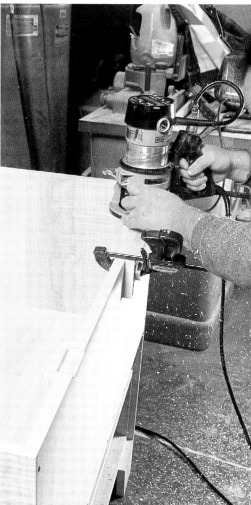

step 3 *The drawers are assembled in traditional Shaker fashion using half-blind dovetails on the front — but that doesn't mean you can't cheat on what tools you use. After you mark and cut the pins on the fronts, the band saw makes quick work of what would have been a lot of hand-cutting to create the tails.*

step 4 *With the hinge blocks glued in place against the cabinet back, mark the hinge shape on the top of the block and the back. Next rout out the hinge mortise to the full depth of both hinge leaves.*

lip on the bottom edge. The dovetail joint attaches to the rear of the lip formed by the rabbets. To keep the work traditional, the drawer bottoms are made from ¾"-thick solid wood, and the three sides of the bottom are beveled to reduce the thickness in order to slide into the ¼" × ¼" grooves in the sides and drawer fronts. Next tack the bottom into the drawer back to square up the drawer.

Some final hardware and you're ready to finish the piece. Check the instructions (if any) on mounting the chest lock and install the locking hardware. Drill and attach the knobs to the drawers.

To give the piece an appropriate 19th-century finish, I used J.E. Moser's Early American Cherry aniline dye and applied a couple of coats of lacquer to protect it.

My wife isn't always happy with the number of magazine subscriptions I have. But when I can turn up an idea like this chest from a magazine ad, I'm allowed to keep those subscriptions current.

ROADHOUSE
PIPE BOX

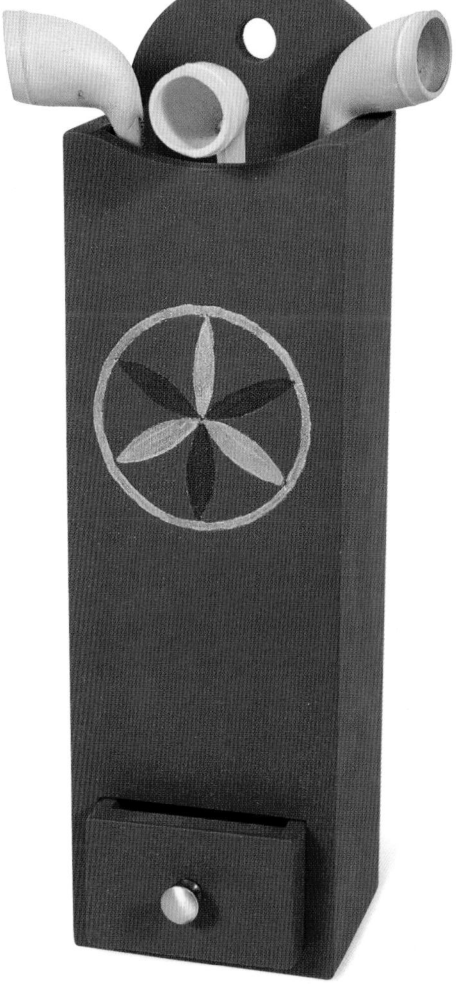

Back in the days of horse and buggy, travelers would stop at a roadhouse, where they'd likely see a box like this on the wall. It held a selection of clay pipes for the use of patrons. A traveler who wanted a smoke would take a pipe from the box and break off a short piece of the stem as a sanitary measure. After use, the pipe was put back in the box for the next smoker. This accounts for the unusually long stems on clay pipes.

If you don't smoke, you could always use this box to hold dried flowers or other decorative items.

Construction is simple. The front, divider and bottom are captured between the sides and attached with glue and nails. That assembly is then glued and nailed to the back. Begin by cutting out all the pieces according to the sizes in the Schedule of Materials. Glue and nail the divider perpendicular and flush to the bottom of the front.

Now glue and nail the sides to the front, flush to the top of the front. Glue and nail the bottom in place.

Cut a radius on the back according to the diagram, then drill a ½" hole for hanging on the wall. Before attaching the back, paint the inside of the box. Mask the edges of the back where the sides meet and paint it also. After the paint dries, remove the tape from the back and glue and nail the back to the box assembly.

The drawer is tricky only in that it is so small. Before assembly, cut a ¼" × ⅛" rabbet on one edge of all four drawer sides. This will capture the bottom. Cut a ¼" × ¼" rabbet into three edges of the front. Nail the sides into this rabbet. Nail the back between the sides and nail the bottom into the rabbet on the bottom edges.

After fitting the drawer to the opening, sand and paint all the parts. Lay out the decorative design using the pattern and a compass. Use a contrasting paint to highlight the design. Attach a screw-in pull on the drawer front and you are ready for the next wayfarer that stops by.

Schedule of Materials: **ROADHOUSE PIPE BOX**

No.	Item	Dimensions T W L	Material
1	Back	3/8" x 3 1/2" x 12"	Pine
2	Sides	3/8" x 2 1/2" x 10 3/8"	Pine
1	Front	3/8" x 2 3/4" x 8 1/4"	Pine
1	Divider	3/8" x 2 1/8" x 2 3/4"	Pine
1	Bottom	3/8" x 2 1/2" x 2 3/4"	Pine
1	Drawer front	3/8" x 1 3/4" x 2 3/4"	Pine
2	Drawer sides	1/4" x 1 3/4" x 2 3/8"	Pine
1	Drawer back	1/4" x 1 3/4" x 2 1/4"	Pine
1	Drawer bottom	1/4" x 2 1/4" x 2 1/2"	Plywood

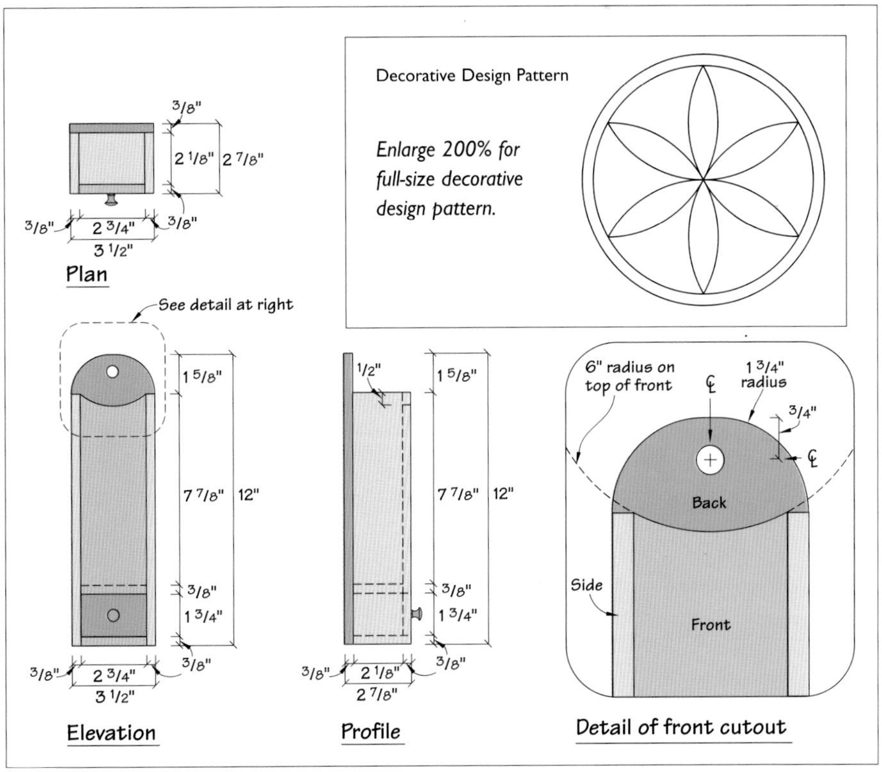
Decorative Design Pattern
Enlarge 200% for full-size decorative design pattern.
Plan
3/8"
2 1/8"
2 7/8"
2 3/4"
3 1/2"
See detail at right
Elevation
1 5/8"
7 7/8"
12"
1 3/4"
Profile
1/2"
2 1/8"
Detail of front cutout
6" radius on top of front
1 3/4" radius
3/4"
Back
Side
Front

Dress up your dining room with this Southern delicacy that was used to serve drinks after a hunt. Breeches and jodhpurs are optional.

SIX-LEGGED
HUNTBOARD

My dad has been making this six-legged huntboard for a number of years now, and it always sells well at the furniture shows we attend. One year he built one for a woman who requested glass knobs on the piece. As most business people know, the customer is always right. Though we weren't sure the glass knobs were right for this piece, we took that huntboard with us to a show to solicit sales anyway. Our first sale that day was for the huntboard. But there was one request: "Could you put some different handles on it?" I'm happy to present here a classic six-legged huntboard with the handles we usually put on the piece.

Quick Tapers for the Legs

The joinery on the huntboard is predominantly mortise and tenon, with all the rails and panels attached to the legs with tenons. The inner partitions are dadoed into the solid back and tenoned into the center legs. Start construction by cutting the legs to size according to the Schedule of Materials.

Each leg is tapered to 1" at the floor,

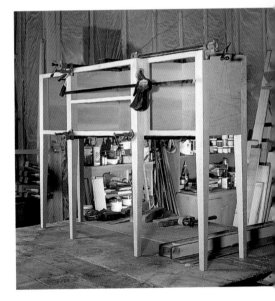

starting 16" down from the top of the leg. The four corner legs are tapered on the two inside edges, but just to make it so you can't use one tapering jig setup (and because it's historically correct), the two middle legs are tapered on the back and both sides. I use a simple tapering jig on my table saw for the four corner legs. Rather than make a new jig for the middle legs, I mark their tapers, cut them 1⁄16" proud on the band saw, then run them over the jointer to clean up the cut.

Haunched Tenon Doors

The joinery used in the doors is a little complicated when you look at it, but makes so much sense that once you've done a set, you'll use this method without question.

With the rails cut to size, the first step is to define the shoulders of the tenon. With your rip fence set to cut 1¼" (don't forget the blade's thickness), cut ¼" deep on the two wide faces for the rails and on one edge of the rail. On the final edge, reset the fence to cut 1" and make the cut. This is the haunched part of the joint and will be the outside edge of the door.

The next step is to use a tenoning jig (you can see mine has seen a little bit of use) to cut the cheeks of the tenons.

The third step is to reset the fence to define the width of the tenon. First cut the full-depth side of the tenon, then reset the blade height and cut the haunched side of the tenon (shown).

The last step is to run the groove for the door panel. This same groove process works for the panels in the door section bottoms. When running a centered groove like this, I first make a cut approximately in the center of the piece. Then I adjust the fence and, with a scrap piece, test my cut. By running first one face against the fence, then flipping it and running the other, I am guaranteed the ¼" x ¼" groove is centered on the door piece.

When the stiles and rails are assembled, the haunch left on the tenon hides the groove on the stiles, making it unnecessary to make stopped grooves.

Many, Many Mortises

With the legs tapered, take a couple of minutes to glue up panels for the back, ends and partitions. Set them aside to dry. Next, mark each leg for mortises. Where the panels meet the legs are three ¼" × 3" × 1¼"-long mortises, evenly spaced along the top 15½" of the leg and set so the ends will be flush to the outside face of the outer legs and the partitions flush to the inside edge of the two interior legs. Where the dividers and rails meet the legs, use ¼" × ½" × 1"-long mortises, again orienting the mortises to keep the rails and legs flush to the outside.

With all the mortises cut, unclamp your panels and trim them to final size. Then mark the tenon locations to match your mortises, and go ahead and form the tenons. If you use your table saw for this step, you'll notice that the back is a little difficult to mount in your tenoning jig without taking out a section of your ceiling. I'd recommend setting your rip fence for the 1¼" length of the tenon (don't forget to include the thickness of your blade), set the blade height to ¼" and run the back flat against the table using the miter gauge (or a sled) to support the panel's back edge. Nibble away the rest of the tenon length with repeated saw passes. The rest can be cut with a hand saw.

If you haven't noticed, I'm a fan of solid wood — even on my backs, partitions and bottoms. Along with that appreciation of solid wood comes an appreciation of what solid wood can do when it moves with the seasons. Because of this, trim the width of your tenons on the panels as much as ⅛" per tenon. This should allow room for wood movement. In addition, when you get to the assembly stage, it's prudent to glue primarily the center of the panel, which will allow the ends to expand.

While you're milling the back, set your saw to cut two ¼" × ¾"-wide dadoes in the back to accept the ends of the partitions. Other necessary pre-assembly joinery includes mortises in the back of the drawer dividers for the drawer runners. Mark and cut the two ¼" × 1" × ⅜"-deep mortises in each drawer divider.

How Many Clamps Do You Have?

You're now ready to assemble the case. You're going to need at least four

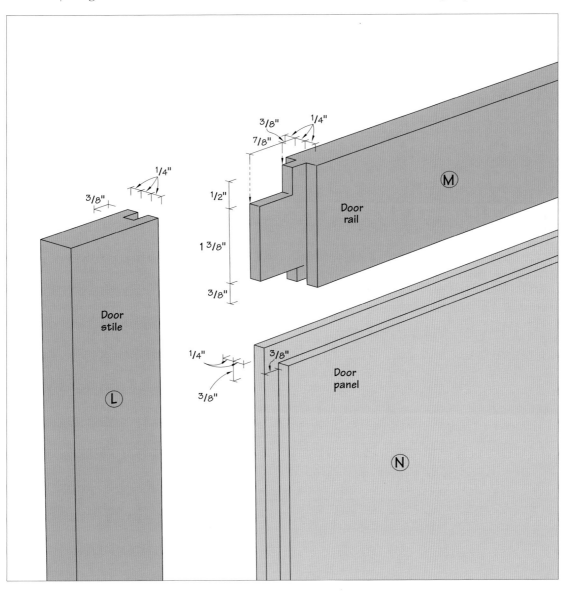

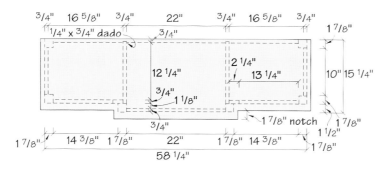

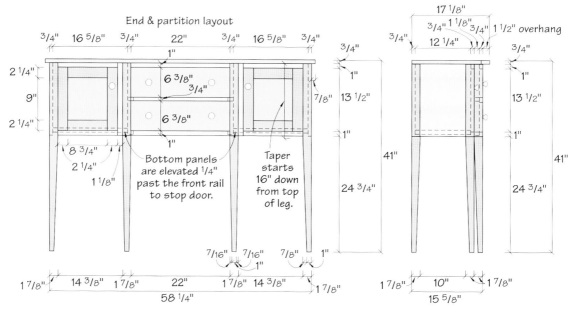

End & partition layout

supplies

Horton Brasses, Inc.
(800) 754-9127
www.horton-brasses.com
2 - Brass knobs, 1¼", #H-97L
4 - Brass knobs, 1¼", #K-12

Woodworker's Supply
(800) 645-9292
J.E. Moser's Early American
Cherry aniline dye, #W14304

Schedule of Materials: **SIX-LEGGED HUNTBOARD**

Case

No.	Ltr.	Item	Dimensions T W L	Material	Comments
1	A	Top	¾" x 17⅛" x 60"	P	
6	B	Legs	1⅞" x 1⅞" x 40¼"	P	
2	C	Ends	¾" x 15½" x 12½"	P	1¼" TBE
2	D	Partitions	¾" x 15½" x 14½"	S	1¼" TOE
1	E	Back	¾" x 15½" x 57"	P	1¼" TBE
2	F	Drawer dividers	¾" x 1" x 24"	P	1" TBE
1	G	Center divider	¾" x ¾" x 24"	P	1" TBE
4	H	Drawer runners	¾" x 1¼" x 14⅜"	S	⅜" TOE
2	J	Door area stiles	¾" x 2¼" x 15½"	P	1⅛" Exposed
4	K	Door area rails	¾" x 1" x 15¼"	P	1" TBE

Door and Drawer Parts

No.	Ltr.	Item	Dimensions T W L	Material	Comments
4	L	Door stiles	¾" x 2¼" x 13½"	P	
4	M	Door rails	¾" x 2¼" x 11¼"	P	1¼" TBE
2	N	Door panels	½" x 9⅜" x 9⅝"	P	⅜" TAS
4	P	Drw. sides	½" x 6⅛" x 13½"	S	
2	Q	Drw. backs	½" x 5⅜" x 22"	S	
2	R	Drw. fronts	⅞" x 6⅜" x 22"	P	
2	S	Drw. bottoms	⅝" x 13¾" x 21½"	S	

Door Section Bottoms

No.	Ltr.	Item	Dimensions T W L	Material	Comments
4	T	Stiles	⅞" x 3" x 16⅝"	S	½ lap BE
4	U	Rails	⅞" x 3" x 12¼"	S	½ lap BE
2	V	Panels	⅞" x 6⅞" x 11⅜"	S	⅜" TAS
4	W	Cleats	¾" x ¾" x 12"	S	

TOE = tenon one end   P = Primary wood: curly maple

TBE = tenon both ends   S = Secondary wood: poplar

TAS = tenon all sides   BE = both ends

There's plenty of work for a mortiser in my shop. To avoid taxing (or damaging) the mortising chisel, make your first two cuts one at either end of the mortise. Then skip a chisel-width space as you move toward the center of the mortise, and come back to clear the space you skipped. This keeps the chisel from bending or breaking.

pine scrap

My tapering jig is simply a couple of pieces of ³/₄" pine screwed to a ¹/₂" piece of Baltic birch. It is built to cut one particular taper, in this case the taper for a huntboard leg, and is inexpensive enough to be one of many tapering jigs I use. Unlike some tapering jigs, the leg is carried on the ¹/₂" piece, supporting the leg from the bottom and side.

clamps, more if you want a quick assembly. Start by attaching the three drawer dividers between the two center legs. Next attach the partitions between the drawer face assembly and the back piece. Clamp this up and set it aside to dry. If you own enough clamps to continue, glue up the two end panels between the front and rear corner legs. The final step is to glue the end assemblies to the back piece, and to attach the door area rails to the mortises in the legs and to attach the door area

stiles. Screw the stiles in place to the back of the middle legs. Predrill a clearance hole and pilot drill the leg to avoid splitting.

Doors and Drawers

With the case assembled, turn to making up some frame-and-panel pieces — the doors and the bottoms of the door sections. I used a half-lapped frame-and-panel assembly for the bottoms in the door sections. The panel is rabbeted and rests in a ⅜" × ⅜" groove in the

rails and stiles. By using a frame-and-panel bottom, I again help alleviate any problems caused by wood movement, while still using solid wood throughout the piece.

The doors are frame-and-panel, as well, but are assembled with haunched mortise-and-tenon joinery, again with a rabbeted panel, with the recessed face showing to the outside of the cabinet. For both the bottoms and the doors, glue only the rail and stile joints, allowing the panels to float in the grooves.

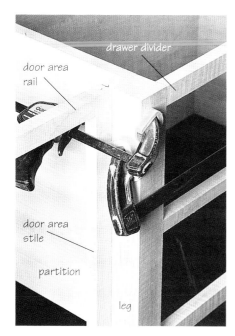

This is the most complicated joinery location on the piece. Shown here is the intersection of the left middle leg with the partition, top drawer divider, and left door section stile and top rail. Once you get a good look, you can see it's simple.

When the door section bottoms are installed they must be notched to fit around the legs. They're attached using ³⁄₄" x ³⁄₄" cleats screwed to the partition and end. Position the cleats so the bottom panel is proud of the door area rail. This allows it to act as a door stop. Screw the cleats in place. Then peg the bottom in place through the ends and partition.

While the doors and bottom panels dry, move back to the case and remove the clamps. To add strength and to enhance the appearance of the piece, I peg each of the mortise-and-tenon joints with squared oak pegs. Sharpening one end of the peg in a pencil sharpener allows me to start the peg in a round hole and end up with a visible square peg. After the joints are pegged, cut them flush and give the entire case exterior a thorough sanding.

When the doors are dry, use the same pegging technique, then sand the doors and bottom panels.

Next make the two drawers. They are constructed using half-blind dovetails on the front and through-dovetails at the back. The bottoms are solid panels raised on the table saw to fit into ¼"-wide by ¼"-deep grooves in the drawer sides, fronts and backs. The groove is cut ½" up from the bottom of each piece. If you do this on your table saw, make sure the groove is aligned properly with the dovetails to hide the groove at the joints.

The drawers ride on runners attached to the inside surface of the center partitions. Each runner has a tenon on one end that fits into the mortises cut earlier in the back of the middle and lower drawer divider. I taper the back end of each runner to make it easier to nail the back end in place to the partition, once the proper alignment is achieved.

Across the Finish Line

The last piece is the top itself. Glue up the pieces necessary, leaving them slightly oversized until dry, then cut the top to the finished size. To attach the top to the case, I use L-shaped fasteners that I make myself. One end of the fastener is screwed to the underside of the top, and the other fits into a slot cut on the inner surface of the case with a router and spline cutter. To allow for wood movement in the top from front to back, don't push the tongue of the fastener all the way into the groove. The front edge of the top is attached by screws run up through the top rails in the door and drawer sections.

Before finishing, attach the hardware for the doors, mortising the doors to accommodate the hinges. Test the doors and trim to fit if necessary.

The finish itself is one I use on all my pieces. I start with a water-based aniline dye. I used J.E. Moser's Early American Cherry on the piece shown here. Once the dye is dry, lightly sand the entire piece to remove any raised grain, then spray the piece with sanding sealer and spray five coats of lacquer.

The hardware that I like for this piece is simple brass (unless someone wants glass.) I used two 1¼" knobs for the doors and four 1¼" knobs for the drawers. Of course, if you prefer a nice glass knob, there's nothing wrong with that. The customer is always right.

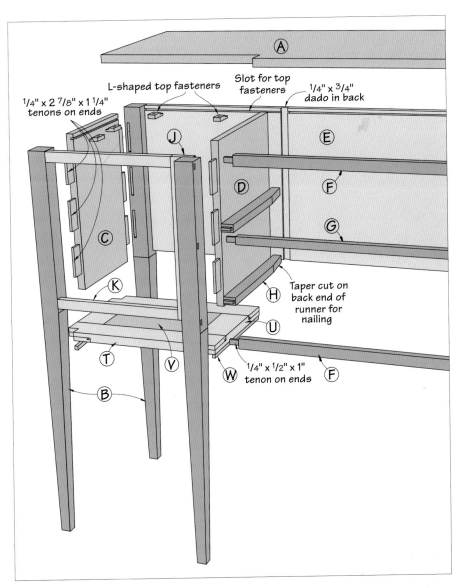

L-shaped top fasteners

Slot for top fasteners

¼" x ¾" dado in back

¼" x 2⁷⁄₈" x 1¼" tenons on ends

Taper cut on back end of runner for nailing

¼" x ½" x 1" tenon on ends

The door section bottom is a half-lapped frame and panel. Seen from the ends, the two frame pieces show the center groove for the panel and the half-lap cut. Below the pieces is the assembled frame.

Happy that I got everything glued up on the case by myself, I'm ready to mount the drawer runners on the inside of the center drawer section.

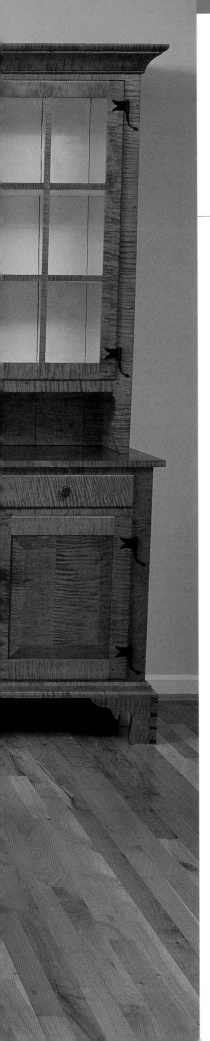

Put your cabinet-
making skills
to the test with
this authentic
Colonial classic.

PENNSYLVANIA
STEPBACK
CUPBOARD

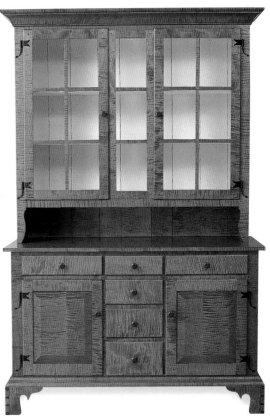

My dad made one of these Pennsylvania stepback units for my mom a few years back, then promptly "borrowed" it to display it at furniture shows. After taking orders to build several like it, he returned the stepback to mom. This piece is now a staple of our business, and we've got construction down to a science.

Approach this project as three parts (base, lower cabinet and upper cabinet) and the task becomes more manageable. The construction is traditional, but not terribly involved. And if you don't think you can construct the muntins and mullions for the glass doors, think again. The way I build the lights in this piece — and all my other glass-doored furniture — is simple and straightforward.

The Base
Starting from the bottom up, the first step is to build the stand-alone base.

The top of it is a simple flat frame, biscuited at the mitered front corners and mortised and tenoned at the rear joint. Form the feet by cutting eight feet halves and milling dovetails to join the corners. The profile for the six visible feet is shown on a drawing later in this chapter. With the feet corners formed, glue them to the base frame

The construction techniques I use in this piece require a lot of mortise-and-tenon joints. I use a shop-made tenoning jig (see the chapter "Table Saw Tenon Jig" for construction details) to make the job less time-consuming.

The loose base is of simple construction but adds a dramatic touch to this piece, being one of the only places where dovetails are visible at all times.

and add corner blocks inside to support the corners. Complete the base by routing an ogee profile on the frame edges. You'll attach the base to the lower cabinet with screws through the frame into the bottom.

The Lower Cabinet

Assemble the lower cabinet from solid lumber using dovetails. Dovetail the bottom between the two side panels, and dovetail 2"-wide stretchers between the sides at the top. The partitions and shelves fit into dadoes in the bottom and sides. Then build and attach the mortise-and-tenoned face frame.

To build the cabinet, start by gluing up the pieces for the sides, bottom and partitions. When your panels are dry, cut a ⅞" × ½" rabbet for the back pieces on both sides and the bottom. Next mark the pieces for the dovetails to hold the sides and bottom together. The two long top stretchers are also dovetailed into the sides, but first they must be mortised to accept the three short top stretchers that are tenoned on both ends. The five pieces then become a top frame to hold the top.

The next step is to build the face frame. The joinery is primarily mortise and tenon, with the exception of two

half-lapped joints where the drawer stiles intersect the middle rail. Cut the half-laps, then mortise and tenon the rest of the joints. Assembly should go as follows: The intermediate dividers fit between the two intermediate stiles; then put all three rails in place; and finally add the two end stiles. Before gluing up the face frame, mark and cut the ⅜"-deep mortises on the back side of the face frame that will hold the drawer runners. After gluing up the face frame, I used square pegs to reinforce the joints.

With the frame complete, dry assemble the cabinet and put the face frame in place on the cabinet. Mark the location for the two center partitions from the location of the drawer stiles on the face frame, holding the partitions flush to the inside edge of the frame opening on the drawer side.

Now disassemble the cabinet and cut the ¼"-deep dadoes for the parti-

tions in the cabinet bottom. Also cut the ⅜"-deep stopped dadoes for the interior shelves and the rear drawer supports.

You're now ready to glue up the cabinet. Start by gluing the bottom between

supplies

Ball and Ball, (800) 257-3711
www.ballandball-us.com
Forged-iron rattail hinges,
#H41-C05, $36.18 per pair

Woodworker's Supply
(800) 645-9292
J.E. Moser's Golden Amber
Maple aniline dye, #W14904,
$10.40

the case sides and the loose top support frame to the sides. Then glue the face frame in place, aligning the drawer stiles with your bottom dadoes. Clamp the face frame in place, then glue the partitions in place.

Complete the case construction by squaring pencil lines from the drawer openings in the face onto the drawer partitions. Follow these when attaching the tenoned center drawer runners in place, gluing the tenoned joint and nailing the rear of the drawer runner in place.

The last step is to glue the notched shelves, side drawer runners and rear drawer supports in place. Set the base cabinet aside for now. We'll build the

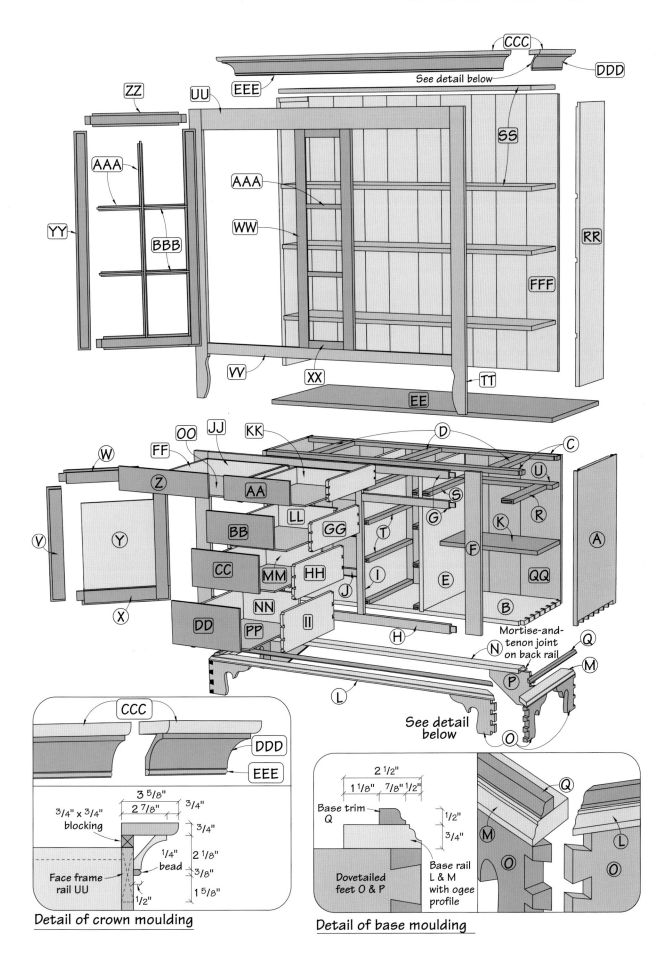

Detail of crown moulding

Detail of base moulding

Simple Door Mullions

Nothing makes a glass door feel more "authentic" than separated glass lights, but the double-rabbeted, notched mullions are never any fun. Here's a simple way to get the same effect.

Working from the back of the door, take two glazing dividers ($\frac{1}{4}$" x $\frac{1}{2}$") and cut them to fit across the door width, seating inside the rabbets in the door stiles on edge. Glue them into the rabbets with a dab of glue so they'll align with the shelves in the top unit.

Turn the door over and cut a glazing flat ($\frac{1}{4}$" x $\frac{3}{4}$") to length to fit inside the door opening from top to bottom. Glue the piece in place with a dab of glue at the two intersecting spots of the glazing dividers already in place.

Turn the door over again and, working from the back side, fit three dividers behind the glazing flat piece, and between the original two glazing dividers. This will complete the $\frac{1}{2}$"-deep spaces for the glass pieces.

Once again, flip the door over and cut the four pieces of glazing flat to fit between the long flat piece and door stile. Glue them to the glazing dividers.

Once the glue dries and the mullions are carefully sanded, you're ready to finish the door and then glaze the pieces of glass in place. I use Durham's Water Putty to glaze because it's easy to work with, doesn't shrink out and hardens to a very tough finish.

The glass I use for most of my pieces is referred to as restoration glass, and is available from S.A. Bendheim Co., Inc., (800) 221-7379 in New Jersey and (800) 900-3499 in California. The mouthblown glass is available in "full" or "light" restoration appearance. Full restoration has more distortion and more accurately replicates glass made in the 17th and 18th centuries. Light restoration more closely resembles glass made during the 19th and early 20th centuries. Call for pricing information.

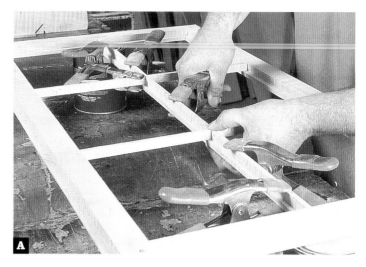

doors, drawers and back after the upper cabinet is complete.

The Upper Cabinet

Start the upper cabinet by again gluing up any panels necessary. The construction of the piece is pretty simple, and much like the lower cabinet. The two

shelves, top and bottom are fit into $\frac{1}{4}$"-deep dadoes cut in the sides. Also milled in the sides are stopped rabbets to receive the back.

With the four horizontal pieces glued to the sides, I again pegged the joints to add strength and decoration, pegging each piece through the sides.

The face frame construction is similar to that of the lower cabinet, using mortise-and-tenon joints to assemble the stiles and top and bottom rails. The one departure is that the center glass section is a separate face frame, also mortised and tenoned. I chose to build this section separately after dealing

The center section drawer runners have tenons on the front end that fit into mortises in the face frame. The back of the runners are simply nailed in place, at right angles to the face frame. The drawer runners in the outer sections are tenoned on both ends and fit into the face frame and rear drawer support.

To make installing the glass in the center frame easier, the frame is built separately and attached to the main face frame with pocket screws.

Fitting and miter cutting the crown moulding is much easier with the upper cabinet turned upside down. Fit the crown first, then add the bead moulding.

with the difficulty of installing the glass in the center section once the cabinet was complete. Leave the section loose until the glass is installed, then use pocket screws through the stiles to attach the section.

Before assembling the face frame, cut the scroll pattern on the inside lower end of each stile. Then glue and clamp the face frame until dry. Once ready, attach the face frame to the upper cabinet using glue and again pegging through the frame into the sides and upper and lower rails.

The next step is to miter and attach the top moulding. The moulding extends 2¾" from the face and sides of the cabinet and will be supported by the crown moulding and bead moulding. I make my own cove moulding by running my stock at an angle over my table saw blade, but you could use stock moulding, as well. Profiles for the cove and bead mouldings are shown in the diagrams.

The top of the lower cabinet is attached to the upper cabinet with screws. After gluing up the boards for the top, simply screw up through the top into the sides of the upper cabinet. When the back is attached it will rest on the top.

With the face frame clamped against the case, I can carefully locate the partition position to ensure the drawer runners will fit in place with little or no problems.

Doors, Drawers and Backs

The doors use traditional pegged mortise-and-tenon joinery, with floating beveled panels in the lower section, and separated glass lights in the upper doors.

Cut all the stiles and rails to size as listed in the Schedule of Materials, then mill the mortises and tenons. The lower doors require a ⅜" × ¼"-deep groove run in the stiles and rails to capture the panels. The groove in the stiles should be stopped to avoid running through the mortise part of the piece. The panels are beveled at an 11° angle on all four edges and should be approximately ⅜" thick, ¼" in from the edge to fit

My homemade knobs and catches take a little extra time, but they make the finished piece feel handmade — as they should (above).

Attaching the rattail hinges is a little trickier than modern hinges, but there's nothing that gives this piece a more dramatic look (left).

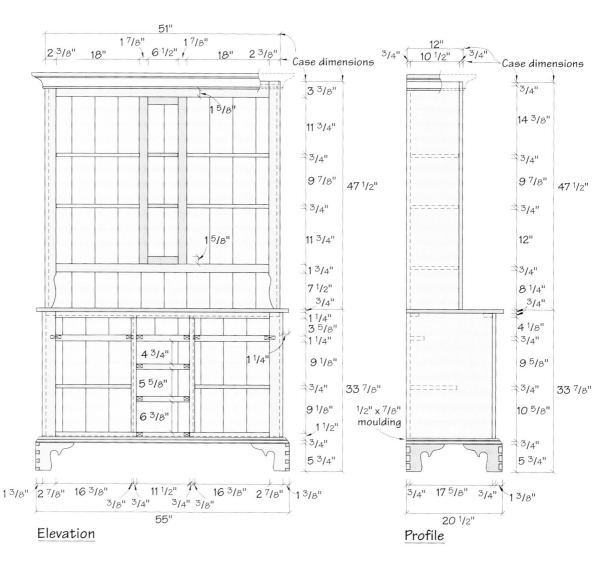

Elevation

Profile

Schedule of Materials: PENNSYLVANIA STEPBACK CUPBOARD

Base and Lower Cabinet

No.	Ltr.	Item	Dimensions T W L	Material
2	A	Sides	3/4" × 18 3/8" × 26 5/8"	P
1	B	Bottom	3/4" × 17 5/8" × 52 1/4"	S
2	C	Long stretchers	3/4" × 2" × 51 3/4"	S
3	D	Short top stretchers	3/4" × 1 1/4" × 15 3/4"	S
2	E	Interior partitions	3/4" × 17 5/8" × 25 3/8"	S
2	F	End stiles	3/4" × 2 7/8" × 26 5/8"	P
2	G	Top & middle rails	3/4" × 1 1/2" × 48 1/2"	P
1	H	Bottom rail	3/4" × 1 1/2" × 48 1/2"	P
2	I	Intermediate stiles	3/4" × 1 1/8" × 25 7/8"	P
2	J	Intermediate dividers	3/4" × 1 1/8" × 13 1/2"	P
2	K	Interior shelves	3/4" × 10" × 19 5/8"	S
1	L	Base front rail	3/4" × 2 1/2" × 55"	P
2	M	Base sides	3/4" × 2 1/2" × 20 1/2"	P
1	N	Base back rail	3/4" × 2 1/2" × 52"	S
6	O	Front & side feet	3/4" × 5 3/4" × 8 1/4"	P
2	P	Rear feet	3/4" × 5 3/4" × 8 1/4"	S
1	Q	Base trim	1/2" × 7/8" × 96"	P
2	R	Drawer runners	3/4" × 2 1/4" × 16"	S
2	S	Drawer runners	3/4" × 1 1/2" × 16"	S
8	T	Drawer runners	3/4" × 1 1/4" × 18"	S
2	U	Rear drawer supports	3/4" × 3" × 19 5/8"	S
4	V	Door stiles	3/4" × 2 1/4" × 19 5/8"	P
2	W	Door top rails	3/4" × 2 1/4" × 15"	P
2	X	Door bottom rails	3/4" × 2 1/2" × 15"	P
2	Y	Door panels	5/8" × 13 1/8" × 15 1/2"	P
2	Z	Drawer fronts	3/4" × 3 7/8" × 17 1/8"	P
1	AA	Drawer front	3/4" × 3 7/8" × 12 1/4"	P
1	BB	Drawer front	3/4" × 5" × 12 1/4"	P
1	CC	Drawer front	3/4" × 5 7/8" × 12 1/4"	P
1	DD	Drawer front	3/4" × 6 5/8" × 12 1/4"	P
1	EE	Top	3/4" × 20 3/4" × 54 1/2"	P
	QQ	Back boards*	5/8" × 51" × 26 1/2"	P

Drawers

No.	Ltr.	Item	Dimensions T W L	Material
6	FF	Drawer sides	1/2" × 3 1/2" × 16"	S
2	GG	Drawer sides	1/2" × 4 5/16" × 16"	S
2	HH	Drawer sides	1/2" × 5 1/2" × 16"	S
2	II	Drawer sides	1/2" × 6 1/4" × 16"	S
2	JJ	Drawer backs	1/2" × 2 3/4" × 16 3/8"	S
1	KK	Drawer back	1/2" × 2 3/4" × 11 1/2"	S
1	LL	Drawer back	1/2" × 3 7/8" × 11 1/2"	S
1	MM	Drawer back	1/2" × 4 3/4" × 11 1/2"	S
1	NN	Drawer back	1/2" × 5 1/2" × 11 1/2"	S
2	OO	Drawer bottoms	5/8" × 16 1/4" × 15 3/4"	S
4	PP	Drawer bottoms	5/8" × 16 1/4" × 10 7/8"	S

Upper Cabinet

No.	Ltr.	Item	Dimensions T W L	Material
2	RR	Sides	3/4" × 11 1/4" × 47 1/2"	P
4	SS	Shelves, top & bot.	3/4" × 10 1/2" × 50"	S
2	TT	Face frame stiles	3/4" × 2 3/8" × 47 1/2"	P
1	UU	Face frame top rail	3/4" × 3 3/8" × 48 1/4"	P
1	VV	Face frame bot. rail	3/4" × 1 3/4" × 48 1/4"	P
2	WW	Center frame stiles	3/4" × 1 7/8" × 34 7/8"	P
2	XX	Center frame rails	3/4" × 1 5/8" × 8 1/2"	P
4	YY	Door stiles	3/4" × 2 1/8" × 35 1/2"	P
4	ZZ	Door rails	3/4" × 2 1/8" × 16 7/8"	P
6	AAA	Glazing dividers*	1/4" × 1/2" × 33"	P
6	BBB	Glazing flats*	1/4" × 3/4" × 33"	P
1	CCC	Top moulding*	3/4" × 3 5/8" × 90"	P
1	DDD	Crown moulding*	3/4" × 3" × 90"	P
1	EEE	Bead moulding*	3/8" × 1/2" × 84"	P
	FFF	Back boards*	5/8" × 50 1/2" × 47"	P

P = Primary wood: Maple
S = Secondary wood: such as poplar
* Cut to fit

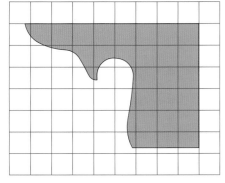

Foot "O" profile

Each square = 1"

snugly in the door frame grooves.

The upper doors are assembled the same way, but require a 1/2" × 3/8" rabbet on the inside edge of the doors to hold the glass. A clever method for making the separate light stiles is shown in the sidebar "Simple Door Mullions."

All the doors are partial overlay, meaning they have a 3/8" × 3/8" rabbet run around the outside back edge. A 3/16"

roundover profile finishes up the front edges.

The drawers also use traditional construction techniques. Cut a rabbet on the backside of the ends to form a 3/8" overlay. Cut a 1/4" rabbet on the backside of the top edge of the drawer front. Then dovetail the sides into the drawer front and dovetail the back between the sides. Fit the bottoms into grooves run in three drawer parts. Bevel the bottom piece to fit in the grooves as you did with the lower door panels. Finally, cut the same profile on the drawer front that you did on the doors.

The back slats are shiplapped, meaning a 5/16"-deep by 1/2"-wide rabbet is cut on two opposing long edges of each piece. The pieces are then interlocked with a gap between the pieces that allows for movement due to changes in humidity.

I used forged-iron rattail hinges to hang the doors. This particular hinge is a little unusual as it's made to fit over a 3/8" lipped door. To attach the hinge,

first locate the leaf on the door so the edge of the leaf is in line with the inside edge of the door rail. Then mark the location for the center hole on the leaf, drill that hole and attach the hinge. Move the hinge so that the rat-tail piece is parallel to the door. Mark the location to hold the rattail in place, drill and screw. Then insert the other screws.

The door handles are made from store-bought pulls mounted on a 1/2" piece of dowel. Then add a piece of scrap as shown in the photo to function as a simple but effective door latch.

For the finish, I use J.E. Moser's Golden Amber Maple water-based aniline dye, a sanding sealer and five coats of lacquer.

Whatever you do when you complete your stepback, don't loan it out for display. I still hear Mom tell the story of losing her new cupboard for a few weeks. Dad just grins and thinks of all the orders we received from that one piece.

Build almost any table you please with these tried-and-true construction methods.

FOUR WAYS TO BUILD A

TAVERN TABLE

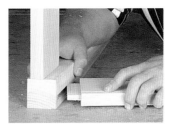

We used to have a table just like this one that was great for playing cards or board games with our two kids. Unfortunately, I sold that table and have always regretted it. So after we finished a couple of new basement rooms for the kids, building a new game table was first on my list.

The top of this table is made from three boards of wormy chestnut, a species of wood that you're going to have to hunt for. I bought mine from a wholesaler who bought it out of a barn in the Smokies. And it was expensive: about $10 a board foot. The painted base is made from poplar.

Begin the project by milling the legs and cutting the taper. You can use a tapering jig for your table saw, but I don't recommend it. A few years ago I came up with a quick way to use a jointer to cut tapers faster and safer. See the sidebar "If You Have a Jointer, Throw Your Tapering Jig Away."

There are a lot of ways you can join the aprons to the legs, from totally traditional to quick-and-dirty. I prefer using a straight mortise-and-tenon joint, though if I were building a little

The plugs for the breadboard ends are made from the same material as the tabletop. Sand the plug to fit, put some glue on the sides and tap it in place.

I usually build my tables using straight mortise-and-tenon joinery. However, there are special cases when other methods are just as good or even better.

side table or something else that wouldn't see daily abuse, the two less traditional methods I'm going to cover would work just fine. But before we talk about the bases, build the top.

Making the Top

After I pulled the right boards from my woodpile, I got them ready for glue-up. I wanted this top to look rustic, so I didn't plane the lumber. Instead, I jointed the edges of the planks and glued up the top. Then I rough sanded it with a belt sander to get it reasonably flat and to remove some of the milling marks. Then I cut the top to size and worked on the breadboard ends.

For a long time I used traditional through-mortises to attach breadboards to cover the end grain of my tabletops. Other people showed me how to do it with slotted screw holes. I was always against using that method until I actually tried it. Now it's the only way I'll attach breadboards. You actually get less up-and-down movement using screws, and the top stays flatter-looking for a longer time. Here's how I make my breadboard ends.

After cutting the breadboards to size, cut ⅛"-wide by 2½"-long by 1½"-deep mortises in the breadboards. I cut five of these for my 36"-wide top. However many you use, it's always good practice to use an odd number of mortises so it's easier to lay them out. I put the two outside mortises ½" in from the end of the breadboard.

 supplies

Rockler, (800) 279-4441
www.rockler.com
• 3" x 4¾" Corner Brackets, set of four, item #34303, $3.49
• Tabletop Fasteners, eight per pack, item #34215, $1.99

These tabletop fasteners are cheap ($1.99 for a pack of eight) and sturdy. Simply place the clip end into the kerf in your apron and screw the other end to your tabletop.

Now cut two slots for two screws in each mortise. I make the slots about ⅜" long to give the top some real room to move if it has to. You can make a router jig to cut the slots, or you can use your drill press and work the bit back and forth. Clamp the breadboard to the tabletop and put two screws in each mortise. I put the screws at the sides of the mortise, not at the center. I do this because I peg the fake plug later in the process, and this keeps me from boring a hole into one of my screws accidentally. Don't drive the screws in too tightly because you want the tabletop to be able to move.

Now plug the mortises. I cut plugs to fit the opening and taper them a bit so they fit snugly when tapped in place. Glue the plugs in place, then peg the plugs through the top with ¼" × ¼" square pegs.

Now age the top. I strike the top with a key ring full of keys; I even write people's names in the top with a knife. It's pretty amusing to watch people as they see me do this. They freak out.

Stain the top with a golden oak color and then add a natural oil finish, such as Watco, which is an oil and varnish blend. You don't want the top to look too shiny.

Now turn your attention to the base.

Mortise and Tenon

Cut your aprons to size. Cut 1"-long tenons that are ⅜" thick. The apron lengths in the Schedule of Materials include the tenons. I cut my tenons first and use them to lay out my mortises, which results in less layout, in my opinion. These aprons are set back ¼" from the front of the legs; this is called a setback.

Now cut a bead on the bottom edge of the aprons using a beading bit in your router. Finally, cut a slot on the inside of the aprons for fastening the base to the top. I use metal tabletop fasteners from Rockler (see the Supplies box on page 54). Rockler sells very sturdy ones, and I recommend them.

For these fasteners, the slot needs to be the width of your table saw's

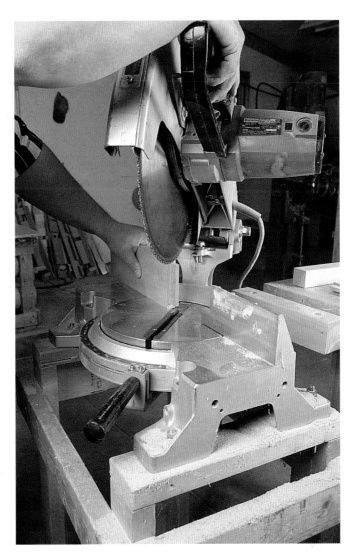

Mitered mortise-and-tenon joinery is common on tables with thin legs or when your set-back is deeper than normal.

When you have to use mitered mortise-and-tenon joinery, don't get too worked up about the fit of the miter. You don't want the miter too tight.

Some Thoughts on Table Design

No matter which construction method you use to build your table, you must follow a few rules when designing your table. Otherwise your family and guests will be uncomfortable: They'll ram into each other, or they'll constantly bang their knees on your aprons.

We've combed several books on the topic of tables, and most sources agree on these guidelines.

TABLE HEIGHT

You don't have a lot of room to wiggle here. Make sure your table height falls between $28\frac{1}{2}$" and 30". A few sources state that 32" is OK, but 30" or less is more common.

APRON HEIGHT

Make sure each of your sitters has at least 24" to 25" of room between the bottom of the apron and the floor. This means that a 30"-high table with a $\frac{7}{8}$"-thick top should have aprons no wider than $5\frac{1}{8}$".

OVERHANG

The distance from the edge of the top to the apron can vary. Between 10" and 18" is great — if possible.

ELBOW ROOM

The amount of tabletop allowed for each place setting should be no less than 23". A roomier table will have 28" to 30".

TABLETOP WIDTH

The standard width is between 30" and 34". A square table for four should be about 40" x 40". Six can be accommodated by a 60" x 30" top.

CIRCULAR TOPS

To seat four, make your top 44" in diameter ($34\frac{1}{2}$" per person). To seat six people, make it 54" in diameter ($28\frac{1}{4}$" per person).

LEG TAPER

Tapered legs are a common feature of dining tables. Legs should taper down to half their width at the floor. The taper should begin about 1" below the apron.

Sources

For more about standard furniture sizes and basic furniture construction, check out the following books:

Rodale's Illustrated Cabinetmaking: How to Construct and Design Furniture That Works by Bill Hylton, Rodale Press, Emmaus, Pennsylvania.

Measure Twice, Cut Once by Jim Tolpin, Popular Woodworking Books, Cincinnati, Ohio.

Encyclopedia of Furniture Making by Ernest Joyce, Sterling Publishing Co. Inc., New York.

Cabinetmaking and Millwork by John L. Feirer, Bennett Publishing Co., Peoria, Illinois.

Be sure to glue the joint and hold the leg and apron together tightly while screwing it together.

Pocket screws aren't my first choice for building dining tables, but for a small occasional table, it'll work.

No.	Item	Dimensions T W L	Material
4	Legs	$2^{1}/_{8}$" x $2^{1}/_{8}$" x $28^{1}/_{4}$"	S
2	Aprons*	$^{3}/_{4}$" x $4^{1}/_{4}$" x $31^{3}/_{4}$"	S
2	Aprons*	$^{3}/_{4}$" x $4^{1}/_{4}$" x $25^{3}/_{4}$"	S
I	Top	$1^{1}/_{8}$" x 36" x 43"	P
2	Breadboards	$1^{1}/_{8}$" x $2^{1}/_{2}$" x 36"	P

Schedule of Materials:
FOUR WAYS TO BUILD A TAVERN TABLE

P = Primary wood: chestnut

S = Secondary wood: poplar

* = Including I" tenon

blade (between $^{1}/_{8}$" and $^{1}/_{16}$" wide) and $^{7}/_{16}$" down from the top of the apron and $^{3}/_{8}$" deep.

Glue up your base, peg the mortises through the legs and finish the base. I use square pegs in my legs. Drill a round hole through the leg and into the mortise. Then take a piece of square stock, whittle one end of it roundish, then pound it into the hole. It should convert your round hole into a square.

Mitered Mortise and Tenon

This method is similar to the straight mortise and tenon above, but you must miter the ends of the tenons because your mortises meet in the middle of the leg. Why would they meet? Well, you might have a thinner leg, or your mortises might be back farther if you chose to use a larger setback.

When this is the case, I make a standard tenon and chop the end off at a 45° angle on my miter saw. You're not trying to match the two miters exactly (it will never show), so leave a little gap between the two tenons. If it's too tight, it could get you in trouble because the ends of the tenons will touch before the shoulders seat into the legs.

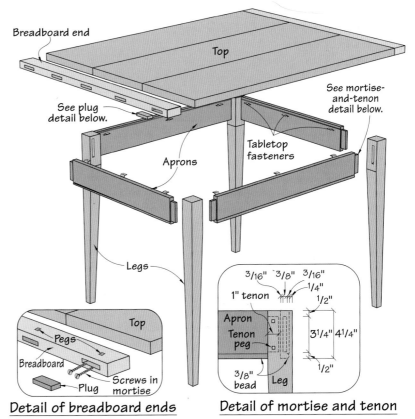

Detail of breadboard ends

Detail of mortise and tenon

If You Have a Jointer, Throw Your Tapering Jig Away

For years I used a tapering jig on my table saw to cut tapers on legs. Even after cutting hundreds of the things, I never liked using the jig. It felt unsafe and always brought my fingers too close to the blade for comfort. One day this method came to me out of the blue. It works so well and so fast that I'm still kicking myself for not thinking of it sooner. It uses your jointer and can cut just about any taper in only two quick passes.

Let me show you how to do this on a $2\frac{1}{8}$" x $2\frac{1}{8}$" x $28\frac{1}{4}$" leg. First mark on the leg where the apron will be. Let's say the apron is 4" wide. Add 1" to that and make a mark 5" down from the top of the leg. Then take the remainder of the leg, $23\frac{1}{4}$", divide that number in half and forget about the fraction — so you get 11". Make a mark on the leg that's 11" up from the bottom of the leg. To reduce the width of the leg at the floor by half (which is standard with leg tapering), set your jointer to make a $\frac{1}{2}$"-deep cut. Now make your first pass on the jointer by slowly pushing the leg into the cutterhead — foot first — until you reach the mark at 11". Lift the leg off the jointer.

Now turn the leg around so the top part is headed toward the cutterhead. Place your pusher-hold-down block on the bottom of the leg and push down so you "pop a wheelie" with your leg. Slowly push the leg into the cutterhead while pushing down and forward on your pusher-hold-down block. When you finish this pass you will have a perfectly tapered leg on one side.

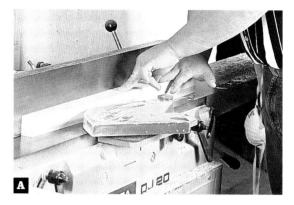

Here I am making the first pass on the leg. My jointer is set to make a $\frac{1}{2}$"-deep cut. As soon as the cutterhead reaches the mark at 11", pull the leg up off the jointer.

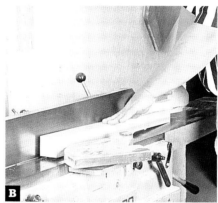

Here I'm beginning the second pass on the jointer. I've turned the leg around and "popped a wheelie" using my pusher-hold-down block. Advance slowly and steadily into the cutterhead.

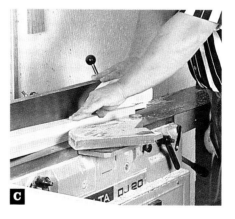

Here I am near the end of the second pass. The outfeed table supports the tapered side after it comes off the cutterhead so the leg moves steadily over the jointer beds as long as I keep firm pressure down on the pusher-hold-down block.

Pocket Screws

I wouldn't recommend this for a large table. If you're going to spend the money on the wood, you might as well do it right. But if you want to build a quick-and-dirty side table, this will work fine. Be sure to glue and screw this joint for added strength. It's important to keep the pieces tightly together as you screw the apron to the leg.

Corner Brackets

Corner brackets are a faster alternative to traditional joinery, but they aren't as sturdy. However, you can't beat them when you want to make a table that can be knocked down and stored away.

These measurements apply to the brackets from Rockler (see the Supplies box on page 54). The first step to installing these brackets is to cut a bevel on the inside corner of the legs. This is where you'll later install the hanger bolts. The best way to cut the

bevel is on your jointer. Set the machine's fence to a 45° angle and the depth of cut to $\frac{1}{4}$". Cut $3\frac{1}{2}$" in on the top corner as shown in the photo.

Now install the hanger bolts, which are odd-looking fasteners that have wood screw threads on one end and machine screw threads on the other. The wood screw end goes into the leg, and the machine screw end is bolted to the corner bracket. To install the hanger bolts, first lay out and drill pilot holes on the leg. Then install the bolts

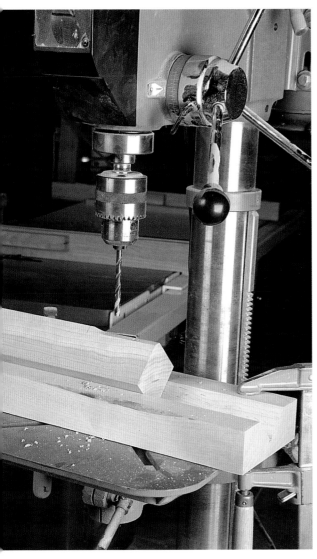

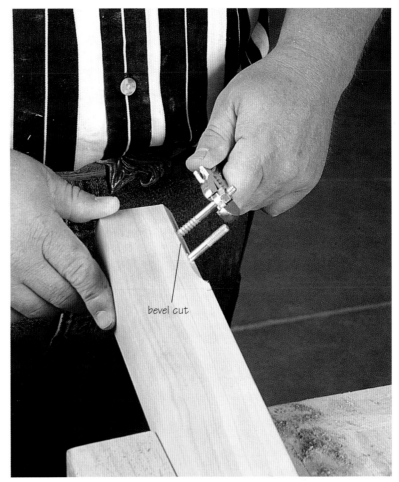

bevel cut

To install the hanger bolts, thread two machine nuts onto the end of the hanger bolt and tighten them against one another. Then grip the two nuts with a wrench and screw the hanger bolts into the leg.

Use the bracket as a template for locating the holes for the corner bracket. Then use a drill press to make your pilot holes.

using the method shown in the photo.

Now you need to cut a kerf in each apron for the bracket to grab. The kerf should be 1¾" in from the end and ⅜" deep for these brackets. Different brands can use different measurements.

Attaching the Top and Finishing

I attach the top with tabletop fasteners that I screw in place about every foot. On the long aprons, don't push the fasteners all the way into the kerf when screwing them down. This will give your top some room to move.

I finish the base with a couple coats of latex paint followed by a glazing stain. Finally, I add a couple coats of lacquer for protection.

kerf for bracket

Corner brackets are great for building furniture that needs to be knocked down or moved frequently.

As I watched my daughter grow, I waited patiently for more than a decade to build this secretary. This year both she and I were ready for this ultimate heirloom.

TRADITIONAL
SECRETARY

Back in 1989 a local sawmill owner passed away and his family went about auctioning off all his personal possessions, including a large quantity of lumber. Before the auction I went through the wood and found some 20"-wide curly maple that apparently had been milled in 1954. I wanted that wood, and so I went to the auction with $1,000 in my pocket ready to bid, but also ready to be disappointed.

When the curly maple lot came up, the auctioneer put one leg up on that pile of wood, spit out a huge wad of tobacco and said the words that would lead to the lumber purchase of a lifetime.

"Who wants to bid on this pile of oak?" he says.

Well, a few minutes and $200 later, that pile of the most amazing and wide curly maple was mine. For more than 10 years that lumber has sat in my shop. I've used a couple small pieces for important projects, but mostly I've been saving it for something very special: a drop-lid secretary for my daughter.

Now, I've been a professional cabinetmaker for a long time and have built just about every piece of reproduction

furniture imaginable. But I've got to tell you that some aspects of this project were a real challenge. The beaded mullioned doors require a lot of tricky cuts that are dangerous if not executed carefully. If you're squeamish, I'd recommend you make the mullions flat instead of beaded. Most of all, don't get into a hurry with this project. It's going to take you a lot longer than you expect.

Lower Case

Some cabinetmakers build a separate base that the case rests on. After years of building Shaker and 18th-century American furniture, I've found it's better to build the lower case and base as one. Instead of a separate base, I make my side pieces extend to the floor and attach the ogee feet to the sides and a buildup block on the front. We'll get to the feet later, but don't look for parts for a separate base.

The lower case is held together by mortised-and-tenoned framed panels that are attached to the two sides using sliding dovetails. The writing surface is also attached to the sides using sliding dovetails. And the top of the lower case is attached using half-blind dovetails. The lid is supported by two pieces that

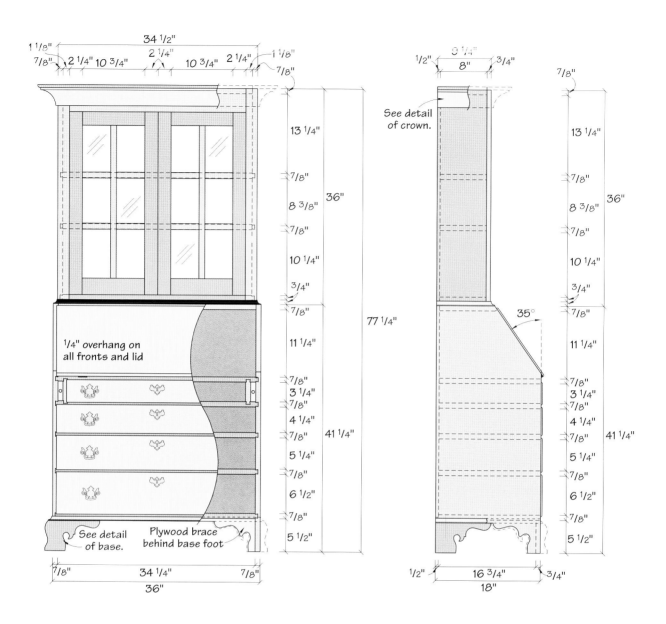

1 1/8" 34 1/2" 1 1/8"
7/8" 2 1/4" 10 3/4" 2 1/4" 10 3/4" 2 1/4" 7/8"

13 1/4"

7/8"

8 3/8" 36"

7/8"

10 1/4"

3/4"

7/8"

77 1/4"

1/4" overhang on all fronts and lid

11 1/4"

7/8"
3 1/4"
7/8"

4 1/4"

7/8" 41 1/4"

5 1/4"

7/8"

6 1/2"

7/8"

See detail of base.

Plywood brace behind base foot

5 1/2"

7/8" 34 1/4" 7/8"
36"

1/2" 9 1/4" 3/4"
8"

See detail of crown.

7/8"

13 1/4"

7/8"

8 3/8" 36"

7/8"

10 1/4"

3/4"

7/8"

35°

11 1/4"

7/8"
3 1/4"
7/8"

4 1/4"

7/8" 41 1/4"

5 1/4"

7/8"

6 1/2"

7/8"

5 1/2"

1/2" 16 3/4" 3/4"
18"

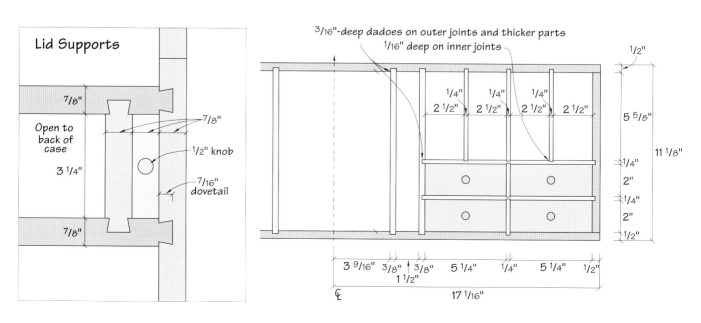

Lid Supports

7/8"

Open to back of case

3 1/4"

7/8"

7/8"

1/2" knob

7/16" dovetail

7/8"

3/16"-deep dadoes on outer joints and thicker parts
1/16" deep on inner joints

1/2"

1/4" 1/4" 1/4"
2 1/2" 2 1/2" 2 1/2" 2 1/2"

5 5/8"

11 1/8"

1/4"

2"

1/4"

2"

1/2"

3 9/16" 3/8" 3/8" 5 1/4" 1/4" 5 1/4" 1/2"
1 1/2"
17 1/16"

Schedule of Materials: **TRADITIONAL SECRETARY**

Upper Case

No.	Item	Dimensions T W L	Material
2	Sides	$\frac{7}{8}$" x $8\frac{1}{2}$" x 36"	P
4	Shelves and top	$\frac{7}{8}$" x 8" x $33\frac{5}{8}$"	P
2	Face frame stiles	$\frac{3}{4}$" x 2" x 36"	P
1	Face frame top rail	$\frac{3}{4}$" x 4" x $32\frac{1}{2}$"	P
1	Face frame bot. rail	$\frac{3}{4}$" x $1\frac{1}{2}$" x $32\frac{1}{2}$"	P
	Back	$\frac{1}{2}$" x $33\frac{1}{2}$" x 36"	S
	Cove moulding	$\frac{7}{8}$" x $4\frac{1}{2}$" x $6\frac{1}{2}$'	P
	Moulding cap	$\frac{1}{2}$" x $4\frac{1}{4}$" x $6\frac{1}{2}$'	P

Lower Case Drawers

No.	Item	Dimensions T W L	Material
1	Front A	$\frac{7}{8}$" x 7" x $34\frac{3}{4}$"	P
1	Front B	$\frac{7}{8}$" x $5\frac{3}{4}$" x $34\frac{3}{4}$"	P
1	Front C	$\frac{7}{8}$" x $4\frac{3}{4}$" x $34\frac{3}{4}$"	P
1	Front D	$\frac{7}{8}$" x $3\frac{3}{4}$" x $31\frac{1}{4}$"	P
2	Sides A	$\frac{1}{2}$" x $6\frac{3}{8}$" x $17\frac{1}{4}$"	S
2	Sides B	$\frac{1}{2}$" x $5\frac{1}{8}$" x $17\frac{1}{4}$"	S
2	Sides C	$\frac{1}{2}$" x $4\frac{1}{8}$" x $17\frac{1}{4}$"	S
2	Sides D	$\frac{1}{2}$" x $3\frac{1}{8}$" x $17\frac{1}{4}$"	S
1	Back A	$\frac{1}{2}$" x $5\frac{3}{8}$" x $34\frac{1}{8}$"	S
1	Back B	$\frac{1}{2}$" x $4\frac{1}{8}$" x $34\frac{1}{8}$"	S
1	Back C	$\frac{1}{2}$" x $3\frac{1}{8}$" x $34\frac{1}{8}$"	S
1	Back D	$\frac{1}{2}$" x $2\frac{1}{8}$" x $30\frac{5}{8}$"	S
1	Bottom	$\frac{1}{2}$" x $17\frac{1}{2}$" x $30\frac{1}{8}$"	S
3	Bottoms	$\frac{1}{2}$" x $17\frac{1}{2}$" x $33\frac{5}{8}$"	S

Upper Case Doors

No.	Item	Dimensions T W L	Material
4	Stiles	$\frac{3}{4}$" x $2\frac{1}{4}$" x $30\frac{1}{2}$"	P
2	Top rails	$\frac{3}{4}$" x $2\frac{1}{4}$" x $11\frac{3}{8}$"	P
2	Bottom rails	$\frac{3}{4}$" x $2\frac{3}{4}$" x $11\frac{3}{8}$"	P
2	Vertical mullions	$\frac{3}{4}$" x $\frac{3}{4}$" x $26\frac{1}{8}$"	P
8	Horizontal mullions	$\frac{3}{4}$" x $\frac{3}{4}$" x $5\frac{5}{8}$"	P

Insert

No.	Item	Dimensions T W L	Material
2	Sides	$\frac{1}{2}$" x $8\frac{1}{2}$" x $11\frac{1}{8}$"	P
2	Top & bottom	$\frac{1}{2}$" x $8\frac{1}{2}$" x $34\frac{1}{8}$"	P
4	Large vert. dividers	$\frac{3}{8}$" x $8\frac{1}{2}$" x $10\frac{1}{2}$"	P
4	Shelves	$\frac{1}{4}$" x $8\frac{1}{2}$" x $11\frac{1}{8}$"	P
6	Dividers	$\frac{1}{4}$" x $8\frac{1}{2}$" x $5\frac{7}{8}$"	P
4	Dividers	$\frac{1}{4}$" x $2\frac{1}{8}$" x $8\frac{1}{2}$"	P
8	Pigeonhole arches	$\frac{1}{4}$" x 2" x $2\frac{1}{2}$"	P

Lower Case

No.	Item	Dimensions T W L	Material
2	Sides	$\frac{7}{8}$" x 18" x $41\frac{1}{4}$"	P
1	Case top	$\frac{7}{8}$" x $10\frac{1}{8}$" x $35\frac{1}{8}$"	P
1	Desktop	$\frac{7}{8}$" x $17\frac{1}{2}$" x $35\frac{1}{8}$"	P
4	Divider fronts	$\frac{7}{8}$" x $2\frac{1}{2}$" x $35\frac{1}{8}$"	P
4	Divider backs	$\frac{7}{8}$" x 2" x $35\frac{1}{8}$"	P
6	Divider rails	$\frac{7}{8}$" x $2\frac{1}{4}$" x $14\frac{7}{8}$"	P
2	Divider rails (top)	$\frac{7}{8}$" x $3\frac{1}{2}$" x $14\frac{7}{8}$"	P
2	Vertical rails	$\frac{7}{8}$" x $\frac{3}{4}$" x $4\frac{1}{8}$"	P
4	Lid support guides	$\frac{7}{8}$" x $\frac{3}{4}$" x 12"	S
3	Lower panels	$\frac{3}{8}$" x $13\frac{5}{8}$" x $31\frac{3}{8}$"	S
1	Top panel	$\frac{3}{8}$" x $13\frac{5}{8}$" x $28\frac{7}{8}$"	S
1	Drop lid panel	$\frac{7}{8}$" x $13\frac{7}{8}$" x $32\frac{3}{4}$"	P
2	Breadboards	$\frac{7}{8}$" x 2" x $13\frac{7}{8}$"	P
2	Lid supports	$\frac{7}{8}$" x $3\frac{1}{4}$" x 17"	P
2	Support ends	$\frac{7}{8}$" x 2" x $3\frac{1}{4}$"	P
1	Feet support strip	$\frac{3}{4}$" x $5\frac{1}{2}$" x $34\frac{1}{4}$"	Plywood
	Back	$\frac{1}{2}$" x 35" x $41\frac{1}{4}$"	S
	Ogee feet	$1\frac{1}{4}$" x 5" x 7'	P
	Cove moulding	$\frac{3}{4}$" x $\frac{3}{4}$" x 14'	P

Column Drawers

No.	Item	Dimensions T W L	Material
4	Front & back	$\frac{1}{2}$" x $1\frac{7}{16}$" x 10"	S
4	Tops & bottoms	$\frac{1}{2}$" x $1\frac{7}{16}$" x $8\frac{1}{4}$"	S
2	Sides	$\frac{1}{2}$" x $7\frac{3}{4}$" x $9\frac{3}{4}$"	S
2	Column backer	$\frac{1}{4}$" x 2" x $11\frac{1}{16}$"	P
2	Beaded boards	$\frac{1}{4}$" x $1\frac{1}{2}$" x 7"	P
4	Plinths	$\frac{5}{8}$" x 2" x 2"	P

Insert Drawers and Door

No.	Item	Dimensions T W L	Material
8	Fronts	$\frac{1}{2}$" x $1\frac{15}{16}$" x $5\frac{3}{16}$"	P
8	Backs	$\frac{3}{8}$" x $1\frac{5}{8}$" x $5\frac{3}{16}$"	S
16	Sides	$\frac{3}{8}$" x $1\frac{15}{16}$" x $8\frac{1}{8}$"	S
8	Bottoms	$\frac{1}{4}$" x $4\frac{13}{16}$" x 8"	S
2	Door stiles	$\frac{11}{16}$" x $1\frac{1}{2}$" x $10\frac{1}{16}$"	P
1	Bottom rail	$\frac{11}{16}$" x $1\frac{1}{2}$" x $5\frac{1}{4}$"	P
1	Top rail	$\frac{11}{16}$" x 3" x $5\frac{1}{4}$"	P
1	Panel	$\frac{1}{4}$" x $5\frac{1}{8}$" x $7\frac{3}{4}$"	P

P = Primary wood: Maple

S = Secondary wood: Poplar

---

slide out beside the top drawer. The back is shiplapped and nailed into rabbets on the side pieces.

Begin by roughing out your parts and gluing up any panels you might need. First cut the sliding dovetails in the side pieces. These cross the entire width of the cabinet side. Build a jig from two pieces of plywood to do this. The jig, as shown in the photos, has a long slot in the top that is exactly the same width as the template guide on my router. The second piece of plywood keeps the jig square to the side. Chuck a $\frac{3}{4}$" dovetail bit with a 14° slope into your router and set the router to cut $\frac{7}{16}$" into the sides. Lay out the locations of all the sliding dovetails on the sides and make your cuts. Now cut the slant on the sides and top as shown in

the diagrams and cut a $\frac{1}{2}$" × $\frac{1}{2}$" rabbet on the sides to hold the back pieces. Do not cut a rabbet on the top piece.

Now turn your attention to the stuff that goes between the sides. Start by cutting the material for the mortise-and-tenon panels that run between the sides. These panels (sometimes called dust panels or dividers) are much like a door, with rails, stiles and a flat panel that floats inside. The tenons are 1" long, and the groove to hold the panel is $\frac{3}{8}$" × $\frac{3}{8}$". When you assemble the frames, glue the front mortises but not the rear ones. When you attach the assembled frames to the case, the divider fronts should be flush to the front of the case and the divider backs flush to the inside of the rabbet. This allows the case to expand with the seasons.

Fit your panels, then cut the male part of the sliding dovetail on the ends of the writing surface, the rails and the ends of the stiles. You'll need to use a router in a router table for this operation. Go ahead and cut the sliding dovetails for the vertical dividers that house the lid supports.

Now sand the back section of the male part of the dovetail as shown.

To attach the top to the sides, I used half-blind dovetails. I cut the pins using the homemade jig featured in the chapter "$19.99 Dovetail Jig." The pins should be $\frac{7}{16}$" deep. Cut your pins and then dry fit the case together. Now cut the tails on the top and knock that into place. When everything fits, disassemble the case and sand the inside of the desk. Glue up the case and clamp it.

Here you can see the jig that cuts the female part of the sliding dovetails. What you can't see is the board attached to the back of the jig (next to my stomach) that keeps the jig square to the side.

Unless you taper the male part of the sliding dovetail, it's going to bind up as you knock it into the case. I made a little sanding block for just this purpose. One edge has the same angle cut on it as the dovetail (14°). Wrap sandpaper around the block and sand both edges of the dovetail. Don't sand up near the front where the dovetail will show. You want that part of the joint to be tight.

Cut the pins in the case sides using a custom-made jig and a template guide in your router. The jig is explained in the "$19.99 Dovetail Jig" chapter.

After the pins are cut, dry fit the case and mark the tails for the top piece.

Here you can see how I build my bases. I add a block at the front and attach the moulding to that. It's much like a kick on a traditional cabinet, except it's flush to the front of the case. Cut out the scroll pattern using a jigsaw.

Cut the tails on your band saw and clean them up with a chisel if necessary.

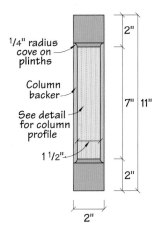

1/4" radius cove on plinths

Column backer

See detail for column profile

2"

7" 11"

2"

1 1/2"

2"

Upper Case

The upper case is built similarly to the lower case. The top is attached to the sides using half-blind dovetails. The two shelves and bottom are attached to the sides using sliding dovetails. Then you build and nail a face frame to the case.

Cut your sliding dovetails in the sides in the locations shown in the diagram using the same dimensions and jig from the lower case. Then cut the pins for the half-blind dovetails in the sides and cut the ½" × ½" rabbet on the sides to hold the back.

Fit the upper case together, then cut the top piece to size and cut the tails on the end to fit into the pins on the sides. Sand the interior, glue up the upper case and build the face frame.

The face frame is built using mortise-and-tenon construction. Cut 1"-long tenons on the rails and 1⅟₁₆"-deep mortises on the stiles. Glue up the face frame and attach it to the upper case with nails.

Finish sand the exterior of both cabinets because the next step is the moulding.

Moulding

The custom mouldings on this project require skill to cut, especially the ogee feet. Begin working on the feet by gluing a long block to the front of the lower case (below the lowest divider). You're going to nail your feet to this.

To make the ogee feet moulding, first make a cove cut down the middle of your stock using your table saw in the same way you would cut cove moulding. It helps to draw the profile on the end of one of the boards to help guide your cuts.

After the cove cut is complete,

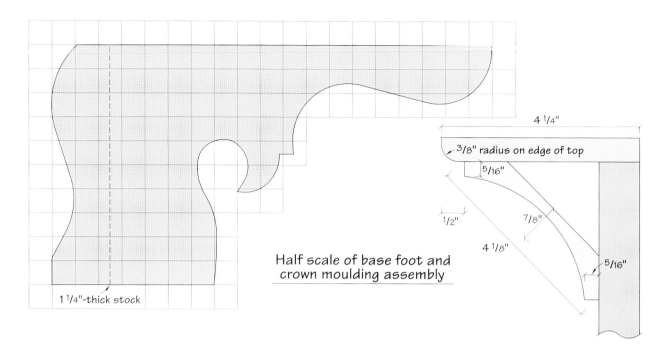

1 1/4"-thick stock

Half scale of base foot and
crown moulding assembly

3/8" radius on edge of top

4 1/4"

5/16"

1/2"

7/8"

4 1/8"

5/16"

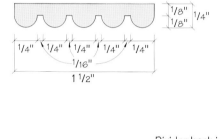

1/8"

1/8"

1/4"

1/4" 1/4" 1/4" 1/4" 1/4"

1/16"

1 1/2"

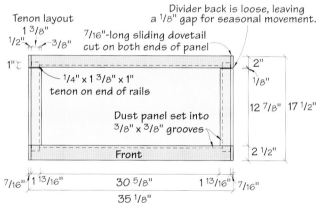

Divider back is loose, leaving
a 1/8" gap for seasonal movement.

Tenon layout
1 3/8"
1/2"   3/8"

7/16"-long sliding dovetail
cut on both ends of panel

1"

1/4" x 1 3/8" x 1"
tenon on end of rails

2"

1/8"

Dust panel set into
3/8" x 3/8" grooves

12 7/8"   17 1/2"

Front

2 1/2"

7/16" 1 13/16"   30 5/8"   1 13/16" 7/16"

35 1/8"

After you've cut out the scroll pattern on the ogee feet, nail them in place to
the sides and the block at front.

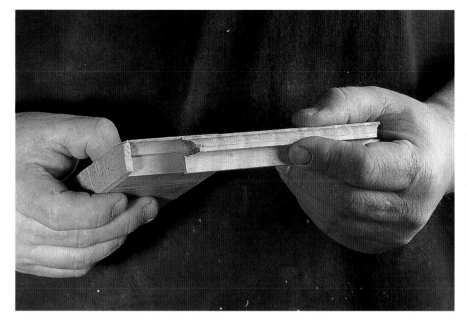

The mullions are tricky. Here you can see the special jig I rigged up to cut the rabbet on the mullions. One edge is shaped to hold the beaded side.

■ supplies

Horton Brasses Inc.
(800) 754-9127
www.horton-brasses.com
• **H-42 ½" interior knobs (10)**
• **H-34 exterior pulls (8)**
• **H-34SE escutcheons for draw-
  ers, slant top (5)**
• **H-38 interior escutcheon (1)**
• **H-551 top door escutcheon (2)**
• **LK-2 lock (2)**

Rockler, (800) 279-4441
www.rockler.com
#29157 hinges for slant top lid
$3.99/pair (1 pair)
#25700 hinges for interior door
$1.99/pair (1 pair)
#31495 hinges for top doors
$5.99/pair (2 pair)
#15190 lock, interior door
$18.99 (1)

Then you simply put the mullion in the jig, set your table saw to make your cut, and be careful.

round over the top of the moulding by running the moulding on edge against your rip fence, changing the blade's bevel as you nibble away at the edge until you can smooth the cuts with a sander.

Sand the feet and then miter the pieces. Trace the profile of the scroll-work from the diagram onto the glued-in block. Cut the scrollwork profile on the block using a jigsaw (it doesn't

have to be pretty). Cut the scrollwork on the ogee feet on your band saw or scroll saw and sand your cut (these have to be pretty). Nail the feet to your case sides and front. Then miter and nail ¾" cove moulding on top of the ogee feet moulding.

You're done with the feet. Now put the upper case on top of the lower case. Center it and attach ¾" cove moulding to the lower case around the

base of the upper case.

Attach cove moulding to the upper case (I bought mine off the rack) and then add a ½"-thick cap as shown in the diagrams.

Doors

The doors are really tricky. In fact, you shouldn't feel bad about modifying the doors to suit your taste or skill level. The joints for the door are formed using a custom cope-and-stick shaper profile. The rails and stiles are attached using loose tenons. The mullions are coped on the ends and glued between the rails and stiles. Coping these tiny pieces is the tricky part.

Begin by cutting the cope-and-stick profile on the rails and stiles. Now cut the cope on the mullions. Here's how: Take a block of wood that's about 4" wide and cope the ends, then rip your mullions from this wider board. Use a really wide pushstick to protect your

When it's all said and done, this is what your mullion should look like. The cope for my set of knives is $^5/_{16}$" deep.

Before you cut your loose tenon joints, make sure all your mullions fit between the door rails and stiles.

Here's a close-up look at the loose-tenon construction. Cut the mortises in the rails and stiles using a spiral bit in a router.

fingers during this dangerous cut. Cut the beaded profile on the edges of the mullions and cut the ¼"-deep by ⁷⁄₁₆"-wide rabbet on both back edges to hold the glass. Because this cut is so tricky, I recommend you use a special pushstick that you can see in action in the photo on page 66.

Fit the rails and mullions between the stiles and get ready to cut the loose tenons that hold the doors together. I cut the mortises in the rails and stiles using a straight bit in a router. Each mortise measures ⅜" wide by 1" deep by 1¼" long. Cut your tenon material from shop scraps. Glue and clamp your doors.

Drawers

The drawers are built entirely using solid lumber. The drawer fronts lip over the case and are rounded over on the front. The sides attach to the front with rabbeted half-blind dovetails and through-dovetails at the back. The bottom, which is a panel with beveled edges, slides into a groove in the sides and front.

Begin by cutting your parts to size and cutting a ⅞₆"-wide by ⁷⁄₁₆"-deep rabbet all the way around the back of the drawer fronts. Then cut a roundover on the drawer fronts.

Cut your half-blind dovetails using the same type of jig you used for building the case. Now cut the ¼"-wide by ¼"-deep groove in the drawer front and sides for the bottom panel. Cut your bottom panel to size and bevel the edges so the panel will fit between the side pieces. Glue up your drawers and slide the bottom panel into place.

Drop Lid

The drop lid is built using traditional mortise-and-tenon breadboard ends. Begin by cutting three 2"-wide × 1"-long tenons on each end of the panel. Use these to lay out the mortises on the breadboards. Cut the mortises a little wide, glue the center tenon in the mortise and peg your tenons through elongated holes in the tenons.

Now cut a rabbet on the sides and top of the lid and round over the front edge like you did the drawers. Attach the lid to the lower case using the hinges listed in the Supplies box.

Build the slide-out supports for the lid. They are simply a piece of maple with a second piece of maple tenoned on the end to hide the end grain. Slide these into their holes and move on to the back pieces.

Back Pieces

I made a traditional shiplapped back for this piece using ½"-thick material. Cut ¼" × ½" rabbets on the edges and then cut a bead on the edges using a ¼" beading bit in a router table. You'll nail these boards in place after finishing.

Insert

The pigeonholes add a lot to this piece. You might want to customize yours with more secret spaces than I did. First build the dovetailed box that slides into the desk. I used through-dovetails because the material is thin. Now use the diagram to lay out and cut the dadoes for all the dividers. I used a dado stack in my table saw for this.

Glue the dividers in place. Cut the pigeonhole scrollwork on a scroll saw and glue it in place using spring clamps.

Build the eight horizontal and two vertical drawers using half-blind dovetails. The vertical "drawers" open to the inside for hanging jewelry. Cut the column profiles and attach them and the plinths to the backer, then glue the whole assembly to the drawers.

To build the little door in the center, I used a cope-and-stick set in my router table. Then I used the band saw to cut out the curve in the top rail, and I cut the profile using the same router setup. The ¼" panel is flat (not raised) and slides neatly into the groove created by the router cutters.

Details

Attach all the hardware and hang your doors. I used an aniline dye to color the piece followed by three coats of spray lacquer. After finishing, attach the back boards and add the glass using either silicone or traditional water putty.

The good news was that my daughter loved the new secretary. I'm sure she'll treasure it for years to come. The bad news is that now my wife wants one.

The support end on the lid support (attached with a haunched mortise), is a nice way to conceal the end grain.

The insert is merely slid into the desk after finishing. You don't need to attach it to the lower case if you don't want to. Here I'm fitting the pigeonhole scrollwork into the cubbyholes using spring clamps.

CORNER
CUPBOARD

I was charmed by the simple, naive design of this "primitive" corner cupboard when I first came across it in Howard Pain's book about the heritage of Upper Canadian furniture*, which is a wonderful collection of antique furniture. The scalloped sides of the upper part of the cupboard make it special in my opinion.

And it's a safe bet the builder of the original wasn't a woodworker by trade and didn't have a shop full of tools. His limited tools give his project something in common with my version, produced in *Popular Woodworking* magazine's "Little Shop That Could" (featured in the book *25 Essential Projects for Your Workshop*, Popular Woodworking Books, 2000). But even my limited power tools would have seemed a miracle to the fellow who built the first one in the mid-1800s.

To construct this pine corner cupboard, I gave my circular handsaw a workout cutting the different angles required, finding this easier to use in con-

*The Heritage of Country Furniture: A Study in the Survival of Formal and Vernacular Styles from the United States, Britain and Europe Found in Upper Canada, 1780–1900 by Howard Pain, Van Nostrand Reinhold Co., 1978

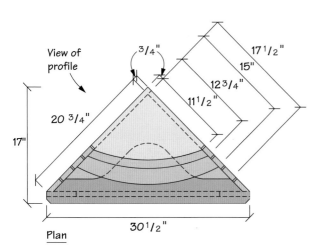

Plan

View of profile

3/4"

17 1/2"

15"

12 3/4"

11 1/2"

20 3/4"

17"

30 1/2"

Schedule of Materials: **CORNER CUPBOARD**				
No.	Ltr.	Item	Dimensions T W L	Material
1	A	Side	3/4" x 21 1/2" x 76 1/2"	Pine
1	B	Side	3/4" x 20 3/4" x 76 1/2"	Pine
1	C	Bottom*	3/4" x 20" x 28 1/2"	Pine
1	D	Lower Top*	3/4" x 24" x 34 1/4"	Pine
1	E	Lower Shelf*	3/4" x 19 7/8" x 28 3/8"	Pine
1	F	Upper Shelf*	3/4" x 17 3/8" x 12 1/4"	Pine
1	G	Upper Shelf*	3/4" x 14 7/8" x 13"	Pine
1	H	Upper Shelf*	3/4" x 12 3/4" x 10 7/8"	Pine
1	J	Upper Top*	3/4" x 12 1/2" x 10 5/8"	Pine
2	K	Front Stiles	3/4" x 4 1/2" x 29 1/4"	Pine
1	L	Door	3/4" x 21 1/4" x 26 3/8"	Pine
1	M	Stretcher	3/4" x 3 1/4" x 28 1/2"	Pine
2	N	Cleats	3/4" x 3/4" x 8"	Pine

* Thickness x width x length of the side of the triangle.

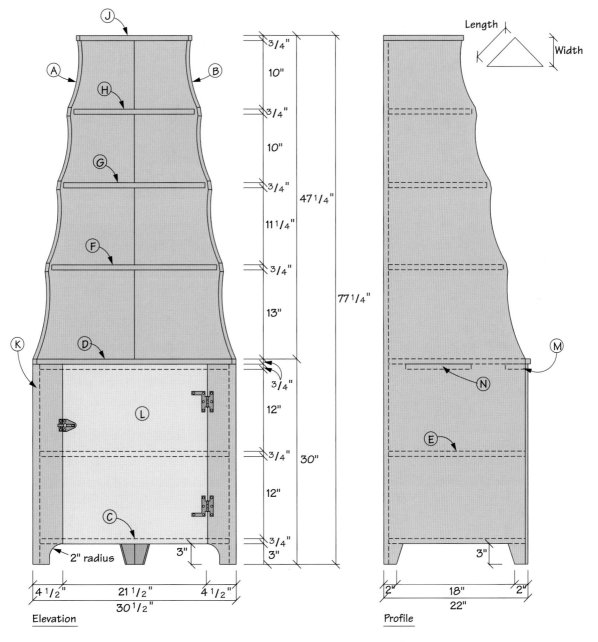

Elevation

3/4"
10"
3/4"
10"
3/4"
11 1/4"
3/4"
13"
3/4"
12"
3/4"
12"
3/4"
3"

47 1/4"

77 1/4"

30"

2" radius
3"
4 1/2"   21 1/2"   4 1/2"
30 1/2"

Profile

Length

Width

3"
2"   18"   2"
22"

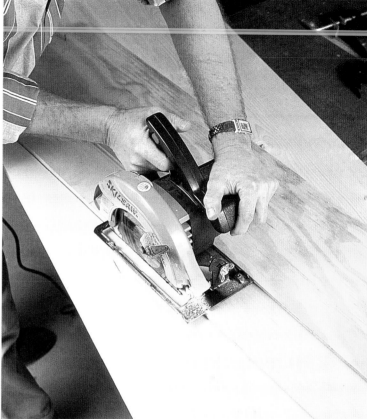

step 1 *Use your circular saw and the straightedge jig to first crosscut for the length of the side.*

step 2 *Then reposition the jig to cut the angle. Use stop cuts where the angle and crosscut intersect.*

step 3 *Use your table saw and clamp an auxiliary fence to your benchtop work table so that you can make the 45° cut on the front part of the sides.*

junction with a straightedge cutting jig instead of my small, benchtop table saw. To cut the curves, I used a compass saw, which left me with a bit of a sore hand before it was all over.

For materials, I bought seven 1 × 12 #2 Ponderosa pine boards that were 8' long. For this project, I figured the knots were part of the overall look.

Begin by reviewing the project plans and Schedule of Materials. When you're ready to head for the shop, the first chore is gluing up three slabs made up of two 8' boards each. Two of the slabs are for the sides. The third is for the triangular-shaped tops, bottom and shelves. I found the "factory" edges on my lumber were fine for edge gluing. Although gluing wide stock together is contrary to sound woodworking principles because of the high potential for cupping and warping, I chose not to worry about it. Again, because of the primitive nature of the piece, this just lends a little more character to the finished piece.

Angle the Sides

Trim to square one end of the two glue-ups. Then lay out the cut line for the angle of the upper sides. From the back edge, measure and mark out a line 21¾" long to represent the width of this side (the other side is ¾" less wide because the first side overlays it in the back corner when assembled). Next, measure up 30" from the bottom at what will be the front edge. Now measure up from the bottom 76½" at the back edge, and in 12" (11¼" on the other piece) to establish the width at the top. Connect those lines and you've laid out the angle from the countertop to the top of the side.

Cut an Angle on the Front Edges

At this point you need to cut a 45° angle on the edge of the lower part of the front of each side. This angle will allow you to later attach the two front

step 4 Here's how to lay out the feet: First draw a line 3" up that's parallel to the bottom edge. On that parallel line, mark a point that's 4" in from the back edge of the side and mark another point that's 3¼" from the front edge. On the bottom edge of the board, mark a pencil line that's 3" from the back of the side and 2¼" in from the front. Connect the pencil marks.

step 5 Draw the shapes of the scallops using a piece of scrap that's thin, straight grained and bendable. Drive a nail at the beginning and ending point of the curve, place the piece of scrap between the nails, then bend it ⅞" back to the midpoint between the two nails. Strike the pencil line and your curve is drawn.

Tips on Screws and Screwing

Clearance holes and pilot holes are fundamental techniques, but they're often not understood by new or even experienced woodworkers. A clearance hole is just large enough for the screw to pass through without the screw threads grabbing the sides of the hole. By allowing the screw to pass through the clearance hole, it pulls the opposing part to it when the screw seats down. Without a clearance hole, the threads are bound in each piece and can't pull the two pieces together when the screw tightens.

A pilot hole, on the other hand, allows the screw threads to grab the sides of the hole. It is usually made about the same size as the screw minus the threads. In most cases, I take the trouble to drill pilot holes when using brass screws because they are soft and prone to break when screwing into thin material that's likely to split, or when screwing small screws (no. 6 or smaller) into hardwoods.

One reason I don't often use pilot holes is because I never use wood screws, opting instead for self-tapping screws, also called sheet metal screws. Wood screws are tapered and act as a wedge when inserted in wood. Without constantly drilling pilot holes, the tapered design leads to splitting, especially in hardwoods. Because the self-tapping screw isn't tapered, and its threads are more coarse (further apart) splitting is much less likely. Screw sizes no. 8 and no. 10 suit 90 percent of woodshop applications.

step 6 *Rout only the curves, leaving the short flat spaces between them square. The 3/8" roundover profile should be routed on the inside and outside of both sides, again, only on the curved scalloped shapes.*

pieces that establish the door opening and the front feet.

Cut the Feet

These feet are made by cutting out a section from the bottom edge of each of the sides. Before cutting out the waste, drill a hole in the inside corners of the cut lines so that you can start your compass saw cut in these corners. Now cut away the waste. Keep your compass saw handy because you are going to need it to cut the scallops on the upper front edges before assembling the sides.

Make the Scallops

Lay out the saw cuts for the scallop shapes following the diagram. You can either make a pattern, as I did, or lay out the shapes on one side only and use your first side as a pattern for the second. If you don't make a pattern, draw the shapes before making the angle cuts on the sides in step one.

Cut the Roundover

It's easier to rout the roundover profile on the scallops while you can still lay the sides flat. So do that before starting the assembly process. Clamp the side you're routing to a table with the edge slightly elevated or hung over the side

step 7 *Make sure the wider side overlays the side that's ³⁄₄" narrower. This will give you sides of equal width when put together. If you screw them together, first drill clearance holes and countersink. I used no. 8x2" drywall screws and placed one about every 18" along the back edge.*

step 8 *Set the blade angle to 30°, set the fence to ⁷⁄₈" and make the first pass with the part facedown and the side of the shelf running against the fence. Run both sides of the shelves. Next, reset the fence to the other side of the blade and position it so the next cut intersects the first at the point of the V. The depth of the V should be about ³⁄₈".*

so that the router's pilot bearing doesn't contact the tabletop.

Assemble the Sides

Begin assembly by joining together the two sides. Do this by screwing or nailing along the back edge.

Cut the Shelves

Most of the remaining assembly involves the triangular tops, bottom and shelves. Start by cutting the pieces you need from the third, glued-up slab you made. The diagram on page 77 lays out the cuts for the best lumber yield. I used my straightedge jig and circular saw to make the angle cuts. In laying out the cuts on the board, be sure you

account for the extra depth on the upper shelves and top that have a radiused front edge.

Also carefully lay out the countertop for the lower section, taking into account the extra width required for the "ears" that lap over the sides at the front. To form the "ears," use your table saw and make a stop-cut on one side. On the other side, you must locate the piece over the lowered blade so that when the machine is turned on and the blade raised, it starts the cut at the desired location near the front edge. Make these table saw cuts first, then use a handsaw to make the short cut with the grain ³⁄₄" deep and 1³⁄₄" in and parallel to the front edge.

If I had a ³⁄₈" cove bit for my router, I would have made the plate grooves in the shelves using it. Instead, I cut them using the table saw.

To complete making the upper shelves, you must cut the radius on the front of two of them and the top, and cut the shape of the lowest shelf in the upper section. To make the curves on the upper shelves and top, use the bendable-stick-and-nails method described earlier. Place a nail at the proscribed side length of the shelf, then bend the stick out 2" and draw the pencil line. Cut the curve with a compass saw or jigsaw.

To make the lowest upper shelf that curves inward, draw lines that are par-

step 9 *Cut the two 45° angles on the ends of the stretcher at the length given in the Schedule of Materials. Screw it in place so that when the ³/₄" countertop is in place on it, the top is 30" up from the bottom of the sides. Place the two cleats the same distance up near the back corner.*

step 10 *Nail and glue the two feet after checking the squareness and consistency of the opening for the door that these two front pieces will create.*

allel to each side 4" in from the edges. Then draw a 3"-diameter circle at the back where the two lines intersect and at the front where the shelf's front edge and the 4" line return back. Now cut away the inside shape.

Attach the Countertop and Bottom

The next step is to attach the bottom and the stretcher and cleats that support the countertop. To attach the bottom, drill clearance holes for the bottom that allow it to set up 3" on the sides, then screw it in place. Attach the stretcher and cleats that will support the countertop. Once done, presand the countertop with 120 grit, then screw the countertop in place up through the stretcher and cleats.

The upper shelves are simply screwed in place through the sides at the locations given in the diagram. The top is placed on top of the sides and screwed down. Once it's in place, I cut back the front corners of the top about ⅜" so they didn't stick out so far.

Make the Door and Front Feet

The front feet have a 2" radius that starts 1" up from the bottom edge and 2¼" in from the outside edge.

The flush inset door is then cut to size and mounted in the opening. I found a nice pair of H-L hinges that, because they install on the outside surface, were a breeze to install. The latch and pull combination matched the style

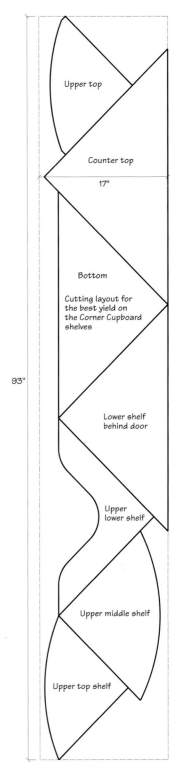

Upper top

Counter top

17"

Bottom

Cutting layout for
the best yield on
the Corner Cupboard
shelves

93"

Lower shelf
behind door

Upper
lower shelf

Upper middle shelf

Upper top shelf

step 11 *After stirring thoroughly, brush on the shellac/color mixture. I applied three coats to achieve the color and protection I wanted. Sand lightly between coats with 360-grit paper. You can sand and apply your next coat after 45 minutes.*

of the hinges perfectly.

Before sanding and finishing, cut the corners of the lower countertop so that they first are square to the front edge and flush to the outside of the side. Then clip the corner at a 45° angle that starts ¾" back from the front edge.

Sand and Finish

To sand and finish, unscrew all the upper shelves and top and remove the door and door hardware, as well. This takes a few minutes but makes the job so much easier that it's well worth the trouble. Give the entire piece a thorough going-over with 120-grit paper using a random-orbit sander. Ease or break all edges, softening them generously.

For a finish, I wanted to add a bit of color without worrying about stain blotching on the pine. That meant a penetrating stain was out of the question. To achieve the color without risking blotching, I used orange shellac by Parks that was already mixed in a can. To the shellac I added brown aniline dye. The recipe is 16 oz. (two cups) shellac and 8 tsp. Tru-Tone brown dye by Dayco. The liquid aniline color is available in many paint stores.

Challenge a friend to
checkers or chess –
or just sit and watch
the world go by.

MILK-PAINT
GAME BENCH

One of the most beautiful stretches of American asphalt is Highway 11 in South Carolina. There, beneath the unspoiled foothills of the Blue Ridge Mountains, you can buy boiled peanuts at the side of the road and browse through antique shops in old barns and lonely gas stations.

One Sunday my wife and I stopped at an old woman's store that looked like it was going to fall down tomorrow. And among her rusted farm implements and weather vanes was this quaint little bench. She told us it was made by the Mennonites in Pennsylvania and somehow ended up in the northwest corner of South Carolina. Now, I'm not so sure I believed the old woman's tale — heck, I don't even know if Mennonites believe in playing checkers. But it was a nice bench. So I built one for my family.

You can make this bench with an absolute minimum number of tools: a circular saw, a jigsaw, a drill and a few common hand tools. Even better, I built this bench easily with two 10' pine 1 × 12s. Total price: $17.98. This bench is a good excuse to buy a biscuit joiner (though dowels work just as well), and I'll show you a trick for these machines that's not in the manual.

Build the Bench
Cut all your pieces to length as shown in the Schedule of Materials. Rip a 1 × 12 in half to make the front and back pieces. Then lay out your clipped corners on those pieces (3½" from the top; 2" in from the side) and cut them with a jigsaw. Clean up the cuts with a block plane or sandpaper. Now cut the hole for the drawer front. Lay out the location of the drawer, drill enough holes to make space for your jigsaw's blade, and make your cuts. Clean up the cut with

step 1 *It might seem tricky to biscuit the shelf to the legs because the fence of the biscuit joiner would get in the way. So take the fence off. Now put the shelf flat on the leg at the exact location where the two will meet. Clamp the two pieces firmly to your bench. Make a mark on the shelf where you want the biscuit to go. Rest the bottom of the biscuit joiner on the leg and cut the slot in the shelf. Now turn the biscuit joiner so the bottom is against the end of the shelf and cut the slot in the leg.*

step 2 *I used an inexpensive paint you can easily find at most craft stores. When masking off the squares, be sure to use masking tape that's intended for painting, otherwise the adhesive will pull up the paint. When the entire board was dry, I rubbed a very light coat of brown glaze over the board to give it an aged look. Be careful not to get glaze on the milk paint or it will turn black.*

a four-in-hand rasp and sandpaper.

Now make the cutout on the bottom of the legs. Lay out the 3"-radius circle with a compass. Or cheat like I did by tracing around a 6" sandpaper disk. Use a jigsaw to make the cut, then clean the edges with sandpaper. Sand all the parts to 150 grit before assembly.

If you're going to use biscuits to assemble your bench, begin by marking the locations for the biscuits. I used biscuits to join the legs to the shelf and the front and back to the top. I nailed and glued everything else together.

Begin assembly by attaching the legs to the shelf with biscuits or dowels. If you're using a biscuit joiner, see step 1

for a trick that makes this operation a breeze. When you're gluing the legs to the shelf, it's tricky to keep your parts square. So cut a narrow piece of scrap to 42½" long. Place this scrap piece between the top of the legs to keep your

bench square while you glue and clamp the legs to the shelf. Next attach the top to the legs with glue and nails, dowels or biscuits. Finally, attach the front and back to the bench using the same method. Clamp everything, clean

No.	Item	Dimensions T W L	Material
1	Top	$3/4$" x $11\frac{1}{4}$" x 48"	Pine
2	Legs	$3/4$" x $11\frac{1}{4}$" x $15\frac{3}{4}$"	Pine
2	Front & back	$3/4$" x $5\frac{1}{2}$" x 48"	Pine
1	Shelf	$3/4$" x $11\frac{1}{4}$" x $42\frac{1}{2}$"	Pine
2	Drawer frnt & bk	$3/4$" x 2" x 10"	Pine
2	Drawer sides	$3/4$" x 2" x 8"	Pine
1	Bottom	$1/4$" x $7\frac{1}{4}$" x $9\frac{1}{4}$"	Plywood
4	Drawer runners	$3/4$" x 2" x $11\frac{1}{4}$"	Pine

Schedule of Materials: **MILK-PAINT GAME BENCH**

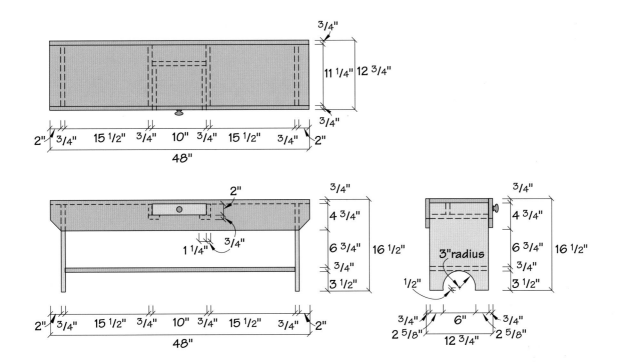

up your glue squeeze-out with a damp rag and allow the glue to dry.

Build the drawer in the manner you prefer. You could simply nail the pieces together. Or you could cut rabbets on the pieces using your table saw. I made hand-cut dovetails just for the practice. I cut a groove in the four pieces to capture the $1/4$" bottom. Assemble the drawer and attach a pull to the front.

The runners for the drawers are easy. Turn the bench over and nail and glue two of the runner pieces between the front and back pieces, flush to the top. These should also be flush to the sides of the opening for your drawer. Now nail and glue the two other pieces to the first pieces so they make an L shape. These second pieces should be flush to the bottom of your drawer opening.

Finishing

This part is more time-consuming than building the bench. I used a blue milk paint for a traditional look (see the Supplies box for a supplier). Once the paint dries, lay out the checkerboard. Mine is 11" square. This makes each square $1\frac{3}{8}$" square. (Buy your checkers from a toy store before you begin building. My checkers were $1\frac{1}{8}$" in diameter.) Lay out the 64 squares using a steel ruler and a scratch awl. First paint the whole board white. Then paint a $1/4$" black border around the checkerboard. Finally, mask off half the squares and paint them red.

Remember that this bench is made of pine, so it's not going to last if you leave it out in the rain. The bench works best on a covered porch — or even inside the house in the playroom.

This hutch can be placed
on a counter or tabletop,
or hung on a wall.

ANTIQUED
TABLETOP HUTCH

This hutch could be used in a variety of home settings, but our reason for offering it to you is as a training piece on creating a simple, but stunning, antique finish.

The wood used for this project should have a reasonably tight grain and be fairly inexpensive. In our part of the country, poplar fits the bill. Start by cutting the pieces to the sizes given in the Schedule of Materials.

Using the template provided, mark and cut the shape on the sides, then sand the edges to smooth the profile.

Next, cut a ¼" × ¼" through-rabbet on the back inside edge of each side, and stopped rabbets of the same dimension on the top and bottom. Stop the rabbets 1¼" from each end.

Now rout the edge treatment of your choice on the front and side edges of the top and bottom pieces. I used a simple ogee bit.

Before the hutch can be assembled, notch the two dividers and the center shelf with bridle joints (also called egg-crate joints) to form the six drawer openings. Lay out and mark the location for the shelves on the sides and nail the shelves in place. Next nail the top and bottom to the sides, slide the divider section into place and nail through the shelf and bottom to hold it in place.

Double-check the drawer sizes against the Schedule of Materials, then cut the drawer pieces to size. I used rabbeted joinery to provide a little extra strength to the drawers. Cut a ¼" × ½"-wide rabbet on both inside ends of the fronts, and another ¼" × ½"-wide rabbet on the back ends of each side. Next cut a ¼" × ¼" groove on the inside bottom edge of each drawer side and front, starting the groove ¼" up from the bottom edge. Assemble with nails,

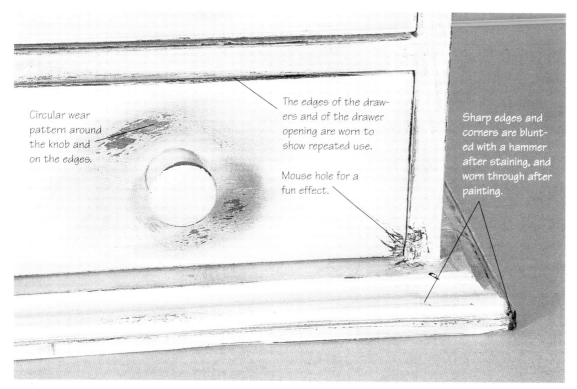

Circular wear pattern around the knob and on the edges.

The edges of the drawers and of the drawer opening are worn to show repeated use.

Mouse hole for a fun effect.

Sharp edges and corners are blunted with a hammer after staining, and worn through after painting.

Shown above are a few results of simple distressing techniques. The stained level of the finish shows through behind the paint, and the paint is worn in areas that would likely see use through the years. The antiquing was done with a gray 3M pad. The mouse hole was done with needle-nose pliers.

holding the drawer backs flush to the top of the drawer sides to allow the drawer bottoms to slip into the side grooves under the drawer back. Leave the drawer bottoms loose at this time.

Cut the hutch back to size and attach the knobs to the center of each drawer. Now you're ready to put an antique finish on the piece.

The finish is a six-step process. The first is to stain the entire piece as it would have been done originally. While this stain will be covered with paint, you should approach it with almost the same care as if it were your final finish. If your final paint color is light, the underlying stain should be dark to provide strong contrast. I used a brown mahogany gel stain on the piece and stained everything, including the inside of the drawers.

Now have a little fun. Use a ring of keys, a hammer or a screwdriver and beat on the piece a little. The idea is to provide the appearance of decades worth of wear, not abuse. It's tempting to go overboard. Think about how the damage you are inflicting could have

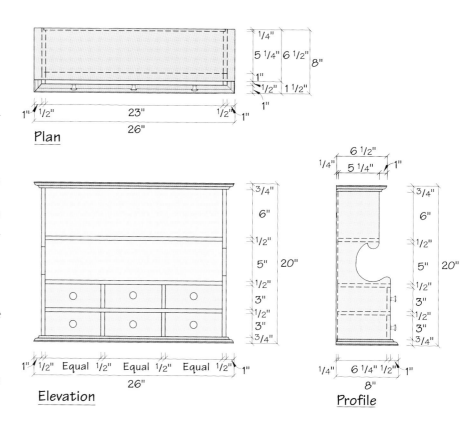

Plan

Elevation

Profile

Full-size profile of pattern on side

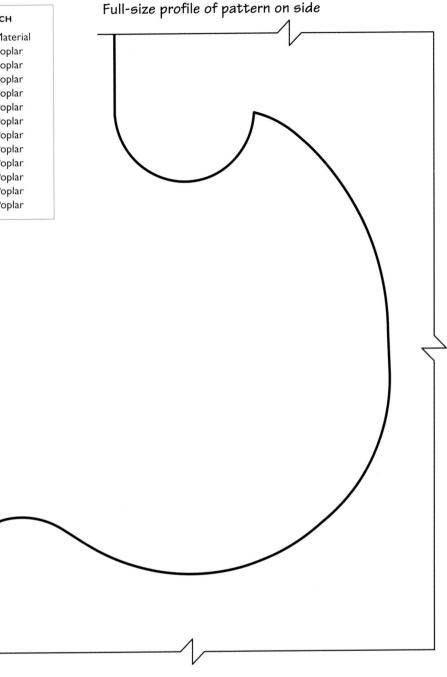

Schedule of Materials: **ANTIQUED TABLETOP HUTCH**			
No.	Item	Dimensions T W L	Material
1	Top	$^{3}/_{4}$" × $6^{1}/_{2}$" × 26"	Poplar
1	Bottom	$^{3}/_{4}$" × 8" × 26"	Poplar
2	Sides	$^{1}/_{2}$" × 7" × $18^{1}/_{2}$"	Poplar
2	Bot. shelves	$^{1}/_{2}$" × $6^{3}/_{4}$" × 23"	Poplar
1	Top shelf	$^{1}/_{2}$" × $5^{1}/_{4}$" × 23"	Poplar
2	Dividers	$^{1}/_{2}$" × $6^{1}/_{2}$" × $6^{3}/_{4}$"	Poplar
6	Drawer fronts	$^{1}/_{2}$" × 3" × $7^{3}/_{16}$"	Poplar
12	Drawer sides	$^{1}/_{2}$" × $2^{15}/_{16}$" × $6^{1}/_{4}$"	Poplar
6	Drawer backs	$^{1}/_{2}$" × $2^{1}/_{2}$" × $6^{11}/_{16}$"	Poplar
6	Drawer bottoms	$^{1}/_{4}$" × $6^{1}/_{4}$" × $6^{11}/_{16}$"	Poplar
1	Back	$^{1}/_{4}$" × $18^{3}/_{4}$" × $23^{1}/_{2}$"	Poplar
6	Knobs	1" diameter	Poplar

happened — corners on the moulding would be dented, edges would be blunted, and the drawers would have seen a fair amount of use. This is only the middle of the antiquing process, so don't go too far.

The next step is to apply a coat of paint to the piece. This would be a point in the hutch's life when it had fallen out of favor and had been relegated to the pantry or cellar. Because of this, the paint job wouldn't be too neat or perfect, but rather an effort to cover the damage to the original stain.

With the paint dry, get the keys back out and add some more "time" to the piece. As a next antiquing step, take some steel wool or an abrasive pad and wear through the paint at points of high contact. This would be around the knobs, where the drawers slide against the top and bottom surfaces of the cabinet, the edges of the shelves and on the edges of the sides.

With the paint finish distressed, add a coat of brown glaze to the piece, immediately wiping most it off after applying. The remaining glaze will leave a discolored look to the paint, and highlight the new dings and scrapes.

As a final step, add a coat of flat or satin clear finish to protect the paint and glaze.

Your completed antique hutch can be placed on a counter or tabletop or can be hung on a wall. Enjoy it, and happy antiquing!

This ingenious box from the early 1800s folds open to reveal a leather surface that's ideal for writing letters.

MILITARY
WRITING DESK

Like a lot of Americans, I've recently been stricken with Lewis and Clark fever. I devoured Stephen Ambrose's book *Undaunted Courage*, watched the PBS special and am now wondering if my wife will let me hike the Lolo Trail. As you probably learned in history class, the primary record of Lewis and Clark's amazing trek to the mouth of the Columbia River is Meriwether Lewis's journal, which was a meticulous account of the flora and fauna they encountered on their trip.

How, I wondered, did explorers write their journals while blazing through the West? I haven't been able to find the answer to that question, but this desk is an educated guess. Traveling writing desks were common among British and American military officers of the day. They wrote their orders and journals on their portable desks, and when it was time to move the ranks, the desk was packed

up and moved with the men.

This desk is an adaptation of a British military officer's desk from the early 19th century. And while you might not be writing orders to your left flank on this desk, it is quite handy for keeping up with all your correspondence. Personal or monarch-sized stationery stores in the area below the top; and pens, paper clips and envelopes fit nicely in the bottom section. Best of all, this project requires very little material. I made this one out of a 5'-long board of figured cherry. The originals were commonly built using mahogany.

Build the Box

The writing desk is essentially a box that has been cut on a diagonal line so that when it opens up, it forms a slanted writing surface. Now, a lot of box makers prefer gluing up a box and then cutting the thing apart on the table saw to separate the lid from the base. That won't work here. Because the cut is on the

supplies

Woodcraft Supply
(800) 225-1153
www.woodcraft.com
• **Hardware kit, which includes all the hinges you need, the chest straps and the lock, #129253, $59.99**
• **Adjustable ball catches, #27H39, $2.50 each**

Woodworker's Supply
(800) 645-9292
• **J.E. Moser's Light Sheraton Mahogany aniline dye, #W1330**

step 1 *I cut my miters on the table saw, though you can use a chop saw if you please. Normally you're not supposed to use your rip fence and miter gauge simultaneously, but this is an exception. Set your saw's blade to a 45° angle and set your rip fence a little longer than the finished length of the board you're cutting. Now mark on your board the finished length of the piece. Make the cut with your saw, then move the rip fence in a little bit until the blade cuts right to the mark. Now turn the piece of wood around and cut the opposite side. Repeat this process for the smaller sides.*

step 2 *This step will mess you up if you don't pay attention. First dry assemble your four sides and mark approximately where the angles will go. Then take the pieces to the table saw. Remember: One side will have to be cut with the miters down against the saw's table and the other side will have to be cut with the miters facing up.*

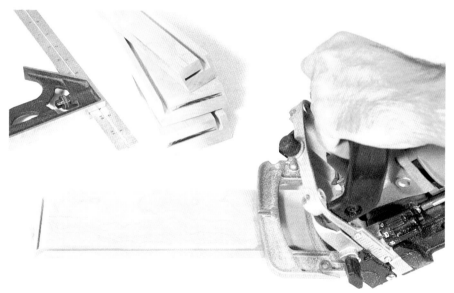

step 3 *Most biscuit joiners have a fence that allows you to cut this joint as shown in the photo. If not, try this trick. Clamp one mitered piece to the piece it will be joined to so that the two miters form a perfect V between them. Then put your biscuit joiner in the V and cut the slot on one side. Turn the tool to the other miter and make the same cut.*

your table saw. The groove should begin ⅛" from each edge. This will recess your ¼"-thick panels ⅛" in from the edges and will keep the panels from rubbing against tabletops. Now cut the panels to finished size and raise them using either a table saw or router in a router table. You want the edges to finish out at about ¼" thick.

Cut the Angles

The trick to cutting the two short sides at an angle is to make sure that the cut begins in the dead center of the back of the board. That's because you want your desk to lay flat when you open it. Set your table saw's tapering jig to 9° and try your setup with some scrap first. When satisfied, cut the short sides.

Now set your table saw's blade to 9° and rip the long sides. This will allow the long sides to mate with the angled short sides. You absolutely must test your setup with scrap pieces before you make these cuts.

Biscuits All Around

Except for two of the corners, a no. 10 biscuit will fit on all of the miters. I used a mini-biscuit cutter for the two narrow sides. You could use dowels in-

diagonal, you either have to build the two parts separately (as I did) or glue up the box and cut the two pieces apart on a band saw that has a generous resawing capacity.

The box itself is simple. The four sides are mitered and then glued together using biscuit joints and polyurethane glue. The top and bottom

are merely raised panels captured in a groove in the sides.

Begin by cutting your pieces to the sizes shown in the Schedule of Materials. Next cut the miters on the ends of the four pieces as shown in step 1.

Now cut the ¼"-deep by ¼"-wide groove along the top and bottom edges of all four sides with a dado stack in

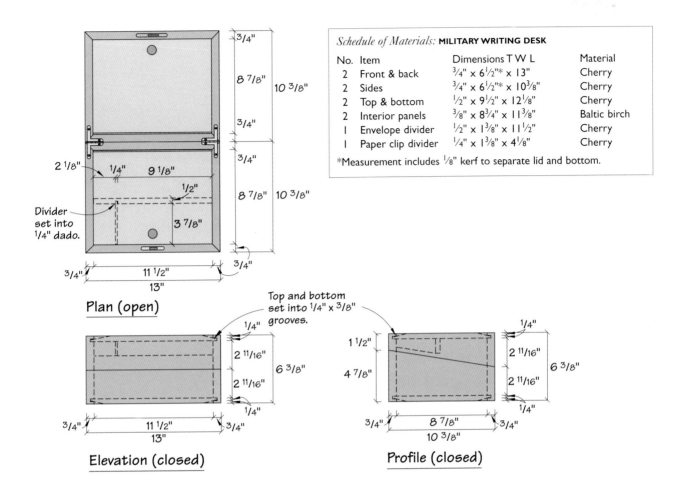

Schedule of Materials: MILITARY WRITING DESK

No.	Item	Dimensions T W L	Material
2	Front & back	$3/4$" x $6 1/2$"* x 13"	Cherry
2	Sides	$3/4$" x $6 1/2$"* x $10 3/8$"	Cherry
2	Top & bottom	$1/2$" x $9 1/2$" x $12 1/8$"	Cherry
2	Interior panels	$3/8$" x $8 3/4$" x $11 3/8$"	Baltic birch
1	Envelope divider	$1/2$" x $1 3/8$" x $11 1/2$"	Cherry
1	Paper clip divider	$1/4$" x $1 3/8$" x $4 1/8$"	Cherry

*Measurement includes $1/8$" kerf to separate lid and bottom.

Plan (open)

Divider set into $1/4$" dado.

Top and bottom set into $1/4$" x $3/8$" grooves.

Elevation (closed)

Profile (closed)

stead. Cut all the slots for the biscuits, then dry assemble the two boxes. When satisfied with the fit, sand everything, especially the two panels and the parts that face inside the box. I started with 120-grit sandpaper and finished with 220.

Some tips for gluing up the top and bottom: First, polyurethane glue is an excellent choice for this short-grain joint. Just make sure you dip each biscuit in water before putting it in its slot and be sure to add a little water to each joint to speed up the curing. Polyurethane glue has a long open time, so you have plenty of time to get your clamps just right. When all of your miters are tight, measure each box corner to corner to make sure everything is square. Let the glue cure overnight.

Now glue some pieces of smooth leather or felt to the two interior panels. Yellow glue works fine. I attached the leather using the same method many woodworkers use to glue up veneer, sandwiching the leather between

two panels. Attach small piano hinges to one of the long edges of each panel and attach them to the inside of the box. Add small stops inside the box to support each panel. I cut a ⅞" hole in each panel so I can easily open the two compartments in the box. To hold the panels in place when you close the box, I highly recommend buying a couple adjustable ball catches (available in most woodworking catalogs for about $2.50 each). Really, though, you also could use almost any other cabinet catch.

Now it's time to join the two boxes using quadrant hinges. Most quadrant hinges have a metal bar that runs between the two leaves to prevent people from opening a box's lid too far. Remove or cut these small bars off; you want your hinges to open all the way. Now attach the chest straps to the outside corners of the box so that when you attach your hinges you've taken into account the space the straps will add. Trust me, it's important. Mortise the quadrant hinges into the top and

bottom. Close the box and sand your joints flush.

Shape and then glue the envelope divider and paper clip divider in place in the shallow side. Mortise a chest lock into the top and bottom. Remove all the hardware and begin finishing. I used a water-based aniline dye and followed that with two coats of clear finish. Then I wiped on a thin coat of warm brown glaze to remove some of the orange color of the red finish. Finally, I added another two coats of clear finish, sanding between coats. This finish, which takes a little patience, gives the cherry a warmth that is worth more than the extra effort.

Now I just have to talk my wife into letting me hike the Lolo Trail. I could bring the desk along and write to her about my journey, my bug bites, my aching feet — all from the same remote and lonely campsites used by Lewis and Clark. Or maybe I'll just stick to trailblazing my backyard.

Nothing says "classy" like bringing out a full tea service on a tray table. Here's all you need to know to build a "proper" tray table that lifts off its base. Butler not included.

BUTLER
TRAY TABLE

When we set out to build a tray table, we thought we'd come across plenty of examples in the historical record. Truth be told, there weren't many. This form probably originated about 100 years ago, in the Victorian era, a time when showing all of the trappings of wealth included having the butler bring out the good tea service for afternoon tea. Having the head servant emerge with everything in its place and setting it on the table base would appear most impressive.

Ellipses and Squares
The top is a rectangle set inside of an ellipse. The wings actually touch at the four corners of the rectangle. With the aid of our computer drafting software, I determined the perfect size of a rectangle that yields equal widths on all four wings. See page 94 for a pattern for the top. (If you want to modify the top and base sizes, you'll need an ellipse-layout jig. See the article "Oval Layout Jig" in the September 1997 issue of *Popular Woodworking* magazine for plans for a simple jig we built to do this job. Back issues are available on our Web site at www.popwood.com.)

Begin by cutting out the parts according to the Schedule of Materials. Next, cut the wings to shape as shown in the photos. Then put the wing parts in place against the rectangle and, using masking tape, attach the wings to the top so they pull up tight.

Mounting the Wings
Mark the hinge locations 4" in from each corner and transfer the location to each wing with a knife. The barrels of the hinges don't align exactly with the wing joint, so use the pattern on page 94 to locate the hinge recesses. Rout the recesses on the table side first; then, with a spacer, rout the wing side. Some chisel work is involved in fitting the hinge's spring mechanism to the top and wings. After this is done, attach all of the wings and test the fit.

You will notice that after mounting the wings, all four can't fold up at the same time. Routing a roundover profile on the edges of the top and wings will fix this. Rout a ⅜" profile on the top and a ¼" profile on the bottom. After this is done, remove the wings. Use a scroll saw to cut the handle holes (see the pattern on page 94), then sand and

step 1 *If you are going to change the size of the top, you'll need to use an ellipse-marking jig. If not, cut out the wing patterns on page 94. Make copies of the wing pattern halves and tape them together. Glue the patterns on the appropriate wings and cut out the oval-shaped wings.*

rout with a ¼" radius. Finish sand the top and wings; set them aside for finishing.

The Pierced Stretcher
The stretcher on this table is strictly for show, and the turned ball centerpiece discourages people from putting anything on the stretcher, including

step 3 *Make a jig to rout the hinge mortises. If you use the hinge supplier that we named, use the pattern on page 94 to make a jig for routing the mortises. If you use a bearing-on-top bit, make sure that you use material thick enough to accommodate the bit and bearing when you make the jig.*

step 2 *Next, clean up the edges of the wings with a block plane and prepare for mortising the hinges.*

step 4 *Begin the stretcher layout by marking the centers of each stretcher piece along the length and across the middle. Drill a small hole through each center and place a small finishing nail through both pieces. Place this assembly on the 60° angle and mark both pieces at the edges where they touch.*

their feet. Rough cut the stretchers to size, then use the pattern on page 94 to lay out the angled half-lap joints on the pieces. I cut the half laps with a hand saw and a rabbet plane, but a straight-edge and a router would work fine. After cutting the half laps, glue the stretcher pieces together.

Next, make two copies of each stretcher pattern on page 94. This gives a left and right, and the crosshairs in the center give a good indexing point. Tape the pattern pieces together and affix them to the stretcher blank, then cut the stretcher pattern out using a scroll saw.

Precision is important here because there is little room for error when fitting the stretcher to the legs later on in construction. Take your time and do it right. Lastly, turn a small ball for the center of the stretcher. Drill a ½" × ¾"-deep hole in the center of the stretcher and a deeper hole in the ball. Attach the ball with a dowel after finishing.

Fluting the Legs
Use a router in a table to flute the legs. Set stops at each end of the fence and measure (include the bit width) from the mounted bit to the stop. The distance should be 1" less

![supplies icon] **supplies**

Lee Valley Tools
(800) 871-8158
www.leevalley.com
• **Eight Butler tray table hinges, #00W21.02,** **($6.50/pair)**
• **Screws, #91Z05.04,** **($3.20/100)**

than the length of the leg. This gives a 1" space at the top and bottom where there is no fluting. Using a ¼" round-nose bit, the first setup is ⅜" from the bit to the fence and ¼" up. The second is centered on the leg. The photo details the setup necessary to complete this procedure. The diagram shows you the location of each flute.

To complete the legs, first set the jointer fence at a 45° angle and cut a chamfer on the inside corner, away from the outer fluted sides. Set the depth of cut so there is an equal amount of width left on each remaining

bevel. See the full-size diagram for details.

Beading the Aprons
The bead at the bottom edge of the aprons will cast a shadow line that separates the aprons from the corner brackets. After beading the aprons, cut ⅜" × 2½" × ¾" mortises on the legs in the locations shown in the diagram. Then cut the ⅜" × 2½" × ¾" tenons on the ends of the aprons. Check the fit with the mortises in the legs.

Assembly and Finish
The base can now be dry assembled to get the finished size of the stretcher. Set the base upside down and lay the stretcher onto the bottoms of the legs, spaced evenly on all four legs, and

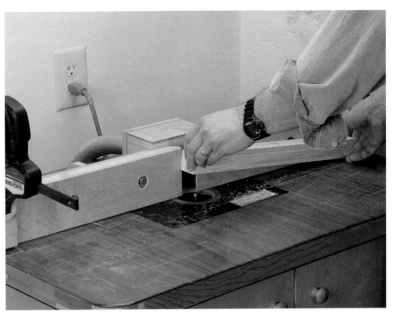

step 6 *With the router running, hold the leg firmly and gently lower it onto the bit with the end of the leg against the first stop (which isn't visible behind my right hand). Run the leg across the bit to the other stop and lift it straight up. Now rotate the leg 90° and repeat the process. Reset the fence to rout the flute down the center of the leg. Use a test piece first; then run the center flute on each leg.*

step 5 *Once you get the angle right, cut the half lap. First I used a hand saw to define the edges, then I used a rabbet plane to hog out the waste.*

step 7 *I beaded the aprons using an old Stanley #45 moulding plane. The bead is a standard ⅛" and can also be made with a beading bit in a router table.*

step 8 *After fitting the stretcher, lay out and drill dowel holes so that the stretcher will attach 5" up from the bottom of the legs.*

mark the joints where they meet the legs. Cut the excess off and sand the ends until the stretcher fits snugly between the legs. Glue the base together and clamp. While the base dries, make eight copies of the corner bracket pattern supplied on page 94.

Lay out the brackets according to the diagram on page 94 and cut their corners square with a miter saw. Note the grain direction for strength. Affix the patterns to your wood and cut

them out on the scroll saw. Sand, then attach the brackets with small brads and glue.

Now build the tray's feet, which keep the tray centered perfectly on the base. First cut 45° miters on the ends of some ¾" × ½" stock (called "Tray foot stock" in the Schedule of Materials) and cut them to 2" lengths. Using the foot pattern on page 94, use the scroll saw to cut left and right mitered pieces for each foot. Place the top and base

upside down on a blanket. Center the inverted base on the top. Nail two of these corner pieces together and attach them to the top at the inside corner where the long apron meets the leg. Leave a little clearance so the top won't get stuck.

Start the three-step finishing process with a thinned-down red aniline dye. Why red? This will accentuate the red that is already in the mahogany. Your goal is a bright reddish or pink color when dry. So don't be shocked if your table suddenly looks like it belongs in the circus. Rag it on, preferably with cheesecloth (it doesn't leave lint on the surface). Wipe any blotches down with a clean rag lightly soaked with the thinner used for your dye. Next, reduce some neutral grain filler with oil-based mahogany stain to the consistency of heavy cream. Rub the stain/filler mixture across the grain leaving a fairly heavy coat. Let it stand for a few minutes until the thinnest part of the application starts to dry. Rub the excess stain/filler out across the grain and finish rubbing lightly with the grain. Apply three coats of clear lacquer, sanding between coats, and you're ready for tea time.

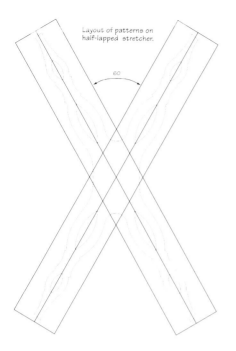

Layout of patterns on half-lapped stretcher.

60

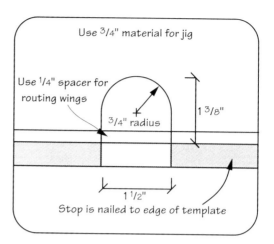

Use ³/₄" material for jig

Use ¹/₄" spacer for routing wings

³/₄" radius

1 ³/₈"

1 ¹/₂"

Stop is nailed to edge of template

Plan diagram of routing jig for tray hinges

Enlarge in two stages. First to 150%, then to 133%.

These drawings need to be enlarged 265% to be full-size. To enlarge them to this size, you need to do it in three stages on a photocopier. Enlarge the drawings 150%, then 150% again, then 118%.

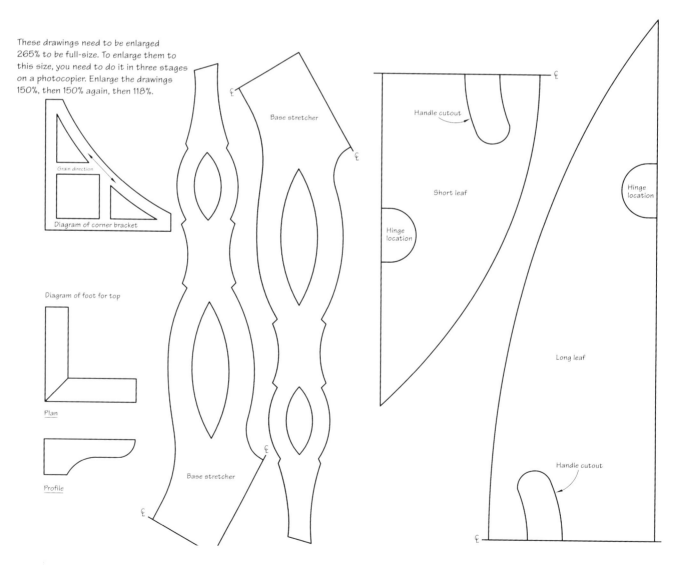

Grain direction

Diagram of corner bracket

Base stretcher

Diagram of foot for top

Plan

Profile

Base stretcher

Handle cutout

Short leaf

Hinge location

Hinge location

Long leaf

Handle cutout

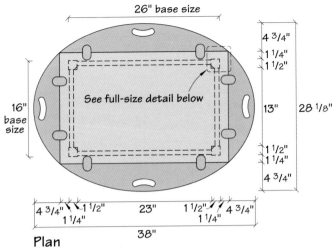

26" base size

16" base size

4 3/4"
1 1/4"
1 1/2"
13"
28 1/8"
1 1/2"
1 1/4"
4 3/4"

4 3/4" 1 1/2" 23" 1 1/2" 4 3/4"
1 1/4" 1 1/4"
38"

Plan

No.	Item	Dimensions T W L	Material
1	Top	5/8" × 18 1/2" × 28 1/2"	Mahogany
2	Short wings	5/8" × 4 3/4" × 18 1/2"	Mahogany
2	Long wings	5/8" × 4 3/4" × 28 1/2"	Mahogany
2	Short aprons	3/4" × 3 1/2" × 14 1/2"	Mahogany
2	Long aprons	3/4" × 3 1/2" × 24 1/2"	Mahogany
4	Legs	1 1/2" × 1 1/2" × 17 3/8"	Mahogany
2	Stretcher halves	5/8" × 4" × 30"	Mahogany
8	Brackets	1/2" × 2 3/4" × 2 3/4"	Mahogany
1	Tray foot stock	3/4" × 1/2" × 24"	Mahogany
1	Center ball	2" × 2" × 3"	Mahogany

Schedule of Materials: **BUTLER TRAY TABLE**

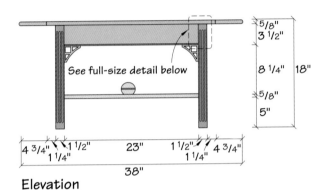

See full-size detail below

5/8"
3 1/2"
8 1/4" 18"
5/8"
5"

4 3/4" 1 1/2" 23" 1 1/2" 4 3/4"
1 1/4" 1 1/4"
38"

Elevation

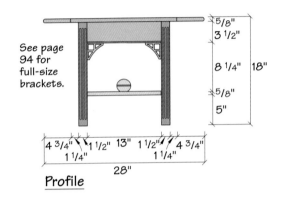

See page 94 for full-size brackets.

5/8"
3 1/2"
8 1/4" 18"
5/8"
5"

4 3/4" 1 1/2" 13" 1 1/2" 4 3/4"
1 1/4" 1 1/4"
28"

Profile

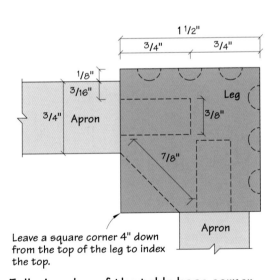

Leave a square corner 4" down from the top of the leg to index the top.

Full-size plan of the table base corner

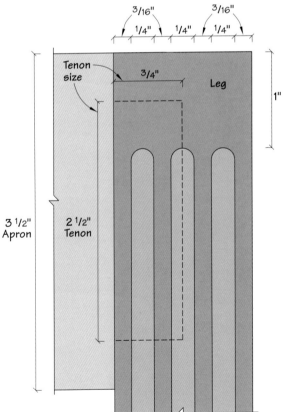

Full-size elevation of the table base corner

95

This primitive and unusual lift-lid desk proves that pine and nails can go a long way.

BURLINGTON
FARMER'S DESK

It was hotter than two rats fighting in a wool sock when Senior Editor David Thiel and I were scouring an antiques show in Burlington, Kentucky, for ideas and old tools. We were buying some lemonade (which, ounce for ounce, was more expensive than premium gasoline) when Dave saw this desk sitting behind an old truck. We should have risked the wrath of our wives and bought it, but instead we made a rough sketch that became the desk you see here.

It's doubtful the person who built the original was more than a casual woodworker, because he or she hadn't accounted for wood movement at all. True, the desk had survived — despite its cross-grain construction problems — but we felt compelled to remedy some of its wood movement troubles when we built this reproduction. However, I just had to bite my lip and hope for the best when I nailed the moulding to the end grain on the top pieces. You could get around this problem with a sliding dovetail, but that seemed silly for a primitive piece.

Construction is mostly nails and glue, although the box is made using finger joints. Then you nail in a plywood bottom and nail the legs into notches cut in the corners of the plywood. The fixed part of the top is nailed and glued to the box. The hinged top is nailed, glued and reinforced with braces to the angled front piece. Nail in some dividers, build some drawers and you're done.

Begin construction by cutting all the pieces to size according to the Schedule of Materials. Cut the two tapers on each leg according to the diagram; use a tapering jig on your table saw or cut them on a band saw and clean up the cut on a jointer. Now cut the ½"-wide finger joints for the box on your table saw. (See the article "Benjamin Seaton's Tool Chest" in the September 1998 issue of *Popular Woodworking* magazine to learn how to make a jig to do this. Back issues are available on our Web site at www.popwood.com.) Cut the angled front out of the front piece with your jigsaw or band saw.

What's "Glaze"? Where Can I Get it?

Because oil finishes reign supreme in many home shops and catalogs (unfortunately), an often overlooked finishing tool is glaze. What's glaze? It's a really thick stain or a thinned paint that you apply between layers of clear finish. Glaze is used by many professional finishers to add depth to the wood or to even out the color among different-looking boards in their furniture. Plus, it's great for creating an antiqued look. Here are two sources for glaze:

1. A professional paint store. Painters use glaze all the time, so most pro paint stores carry it.
2. Merit Industries, (800) 856-4441, www.meritindustries.com, carries three brands of glaze at discount prices.

For more information on glazing, read Bob Flexner's *Understanding Wood Finishing* (Rodale Press).

 supplies

Van Dyke's Restorers
(800) 558-1234
www.vandykes.com
*   **Darkened brass pull, #AG-02305700, $3.95**
*   **Hinges, #AG-02265477, $4.95 a pair**
*   **Knobs, #AG-02219570, $.95 each**

Now fit the bottom. I used knotty pine plywood. Beware: It's so expensive (about $60 for a 4 × 8 sheet) you'll feel like you've been beaten like a tied-up goat. So you might want to buy a decent grade of construction plywood from the home center and sand the heck out of it, instead. Cut four 2½" × 2½" notches in the pine plywood's corners to make room for the legs. Glue a ⅛"-thick strip of pine to the front edge of the plywood to hide that edge when the desk is open. Then dry fit the four sides of the box around the bottom. When you've got a good fit, glue the finger joints together around the bottom. Clamp and allow to dry. When dry, nail the bottom in place (moulding will cover the nail holes). Now glue and nail the legs in place. Clamp and allow to dry.

Next work on the top. Cut the mortises for the two butt hinges into the edges where the two top pieces will meet. Nail and glue the fixed top in place on the back half of the desk. Install the hinges on the two top pieces. Then glue and nail the angled front flush to the front edge of the top that

pivots. Cut out the triangular braces and nail them in place behind the angled front piece for extra support. When everything seems to be working, screw the two battens to the flip top to help keep the pine from warping. Be sure to make the screw holes in the batten pieces elongated ovals that run with the grain. This will allow your top to shrink and expand without snapping the screw heads.

Now turn to the desk's interior dividers. They are joined by ¾" × 4¾" lap joints so the dividers slide together and then slide in place inside the desk. Note that the vertical dividers are cut so that the grain runs from the top to the desk's bottom. This keeps you from seeing end grain on the dividers and stops the divider from eventually breaking the fixed top off your desk. Finish the inside of the desk, nail the dividers in place and then nail moulding to the two top pieces and the bottom edge of the box.

Next build your drawers. I used ¼" dovetails to join the sides to the drawer fronts. Then I cut ¼" × ½" rabbets on the back ends of the sides to hold the back piece in place. The plywood bottom is held in place in a ¼" × ¼" groove in the sides and drawer front. Glue some scraps in the box to serve as drawer stops.

To achieve the dirty-looking aged finish, first brush on one coat of orange shellac and allow it to dry. Rag on warm brown glaze, allow it to sit for about 15 or 20 minutes, and rub off most of it, except in the corners. Allow the glaze to dry overnight. Then cover the entire project with two coats of a clear finish.

Finally, cross your fingers and hope your pine is stable.

Schedule of Materials: **BURLINGTON FARMER'S DESK**

No.	Item	Dimensions T W L	Material
4	Legs	$2^1/2$" x $2^1/2$" x $36^1/2$"	Pine
2	Front/back	$3/4$" x $7^1/4$" x $34^1/2$"	Pine
2	Sides	$3/4$" x $7^1/4$" x 30"	Pine
2	Tops	$3/4$" x 15" x $34^1/2$"	Pine
1	Bottom*	$3/4$" x $28^1/2$" x 33"	Pine ply.
2	Vert. dividers	$3/4$" x $9^1/2$" x $6^1/2$"	Pine
1	Horiz. dividers	$3/4$" x $9^1/2$" x 33"	Pine
2	Braces for front	$3/4$" x 3" x 3"	Pine
2	Battens	$3/4$" x 2" x 10"	Pine
3	Drawer fronts	$3/4$" x $2^{13}/16$" x $10^3/8$"	Scraps
6	Drawer sides	$1/2$" x $2^{13}/16$" x 10"	Pine
3	Drawer backs	$1/2$" x $2^5/16$" x $9^7/8$"	Pine
3	Drawer bottoms	$1/4$" x $9^7/8$" x $9^5/8$"	Plywood
	Ogee trim	25' of $3/4$" x $3/4$"	Pine

*Size includes $1/16$" pine edging

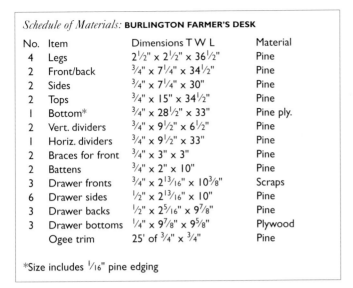

Plan

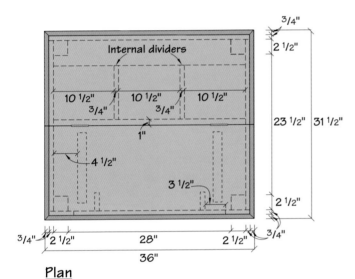

Elevation

36"

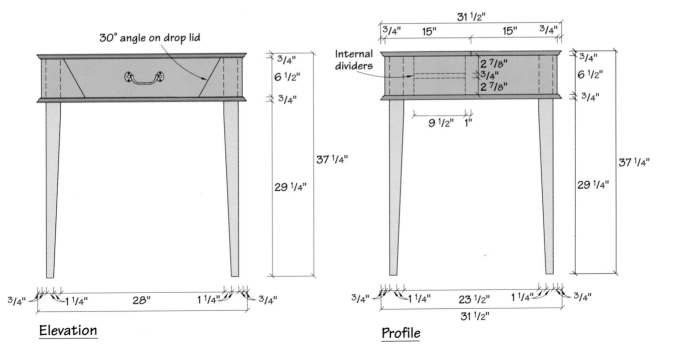

Taper begins 2" beneath the bottom of the desk.

Diagram of leg taper

30° angle on drop lid

Internal dividers

Profile

This classic cupboard
is a nice accent piece
for that empty corner.

SHAKER

HANGING CABINET

I designed this cabinet after seeing a similar hanging cupboard in a book about the Pennsylvania Dutch. That cupboard had a drawer in the bottom and a glass door. After building a copy of that original design, I discovered it was too heavy for my taste, so I redesigned the piece in a Shaker style to what you see here.

The entire piece is made from about 26 board feet of curly maple, a wood that I work with as much as possible. Finding wood with this much figure takes a lot of effort and money — curly maple can cost as much as $15 a board foot. However, you can buy very respectable curly maple for only about $6 a board foot. In fact, you don't even have to use maple. The Shakers used whatever wood was around them for their furniture, so cherry, walnut and pine are all appropriate for this cupboard.

Make the Basic Frame
Begin by cutting the shelves to shape as shown in the diagram. I cut the shelves using a premade pattern and a router, though you might be more comfortable using your band saw here.

Next make the two face stiles. The mortises in these pieces hold the tenons on the curved and straight rails that form the face of the cabinet. Mark the locations of the ¼"-wide by 1"-deep mortises as shown in the diagram, then chain drill the mortises on your drill press and chisel out the waste.

Next, make the 22½° cuts on one edge of each of the face and end stiles. Then make two 45° cuts on the back stile. While you're making angled cuts on the table saw, make the spline cuts. The photo shows the setup for these cuts in the face and end stiles.

To hold the back pieces in place, make a ⅜" × ⅝" rabbet on each end stile. The rabbet goes to the inside of the long edge, opposite the angle cut.

Finally, mark the locations for the dadoes that hold the shelves on the back and end stiles. Measuring from the bottom of the stiles, the dadoes' top edges occur at 2¼", 11¼", 22⅛" and 33⅝". Then use a dado set to make the four ¼" × ¾" dadoes in the stiles.

step 2 *When dry assembling the frame, I use small pieces of scrap with a clearance hole and slip them over the screw to keep the screw or screwdriver from accidentally marring the sides.*

step 3 *The double tenons on the curved top rail are ¼" x 1" x 1½". Make sure the lower tenons are flush with the curve to avoid breaking off the tip of the curve. The tenons on the two other rails measure ¼" x 1" x 1".*

step 1 *Set your table saw to 22½° to cut the bevel on one edge of the front piece. To make the ³/₁₆"-deep kerf cut for the spline, keep your blade set to the same angle, but move the table saw's fence in, as shown in the photo.*

Assemble the Frame

Next dry assemble the shelves into the dadoes in the back and end stiles to check for fit. If everything fits, screw the back stile to the shelves. Then screw the end stiles to the shelves, making sure the bevels face the front. The type of screw here isn't important because you'll later replace these with square pegs. The photo shows this in step 2.

Build the Face Frame

With the carcass of the cabinet dry assembled, cut the face rails to size. I do most of the tenoning work on the table saw, though I use the band saw to cut out some of the waste between the double tenons on the curved stile. Use the assembled carcass and face stiles to mark the shoulder locations on the face

rails, then cut the tenons to size. Clean up your tenons with a chisel and test fit your mortises in the front stiles. The graceful arch on the top rail is cut on a band saw. When everything fits, you're ready to glue the face frame.

Glue-Up

First glue one of the face stiles to the shelves, pegging the dado as shown in

step 4. Remove the other end stile and glue the face frame to the front and first end stile using a ⅛" × ¾" × 34" spline. Then glue and peg the other face stile to the shelves. I also use screws here for extra strength. After the glue cures, remove the screws and replace them with square pegs.

To pull the splined joint together during gluing, I use the homemade clamping cauls shown in stpe 4. Make the cauls by screwing a piece of ¼" plywood to a piece of scrap cut at a 22½° bevel on one side. Take my advice, I've tried clamping these cabinets a dozen different ways. This is the best.

After the glue is dry, remove the screws and peg the remainder of the cabinet, including the tenons and shelves on the front face. This will give your joints even more strength.

Add the Detail Moulding

Though you can buy moulding from a dealer, I prefer to make my own. This cabinet has three pieces of moulding. The top crown is simply a piece of 4/4 maple that has been rounded over on one edge. The piece below it is made by following the steps in the accompanying sidebar "Cove-Cutting." The detail moulding at the bottom of the cabinet is made by routing a classic ogee profile on a strip of ¾" × ⅝" maple using a Freud bit (38-502).

First cut the 22½° miters for all the top moulding pieces. Attach them to the carcass with glue and screws, then glue and nail the coved piece below it as shown in step 5.

Make the Back and Door

The back pieces are shiplapped using a ¼" × ⅜" rabbet cut on one edge of each of the four pieces. Before attaching the back, I like to paint the inside of the back's rabbets black. That way if there's any wood movement, only the black will show, instead of raw wood. I nail the back pieces to the carcass using cut nails for an authentic effect.

The door is made with traditional frame-and-panel construction. Cut ¼" × ⅞" × 1⁷⁄₁₆" tenons on the ends of each of the rails. Then cut the ¼" × ⅜"-deep grooves on the rails and stiles to house the panel. The grooves in the stiles should be stopped ¼" from each end to hide the groove. Next make the grooves in the door stiles a little deeper to form the mortises for the rail tenons.

After test fitting the door frame, make the panel. First cut a ³⁄₁₆" × ½" rabbet on all four sides of the back of the panel. The bevel on the front starts 1⅝"

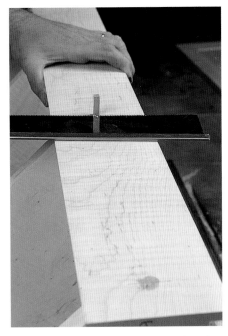
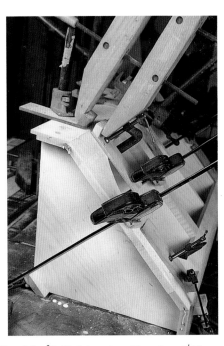

step 4 *Here's how to peg the joints in the cabinet: First drill a ³⁄₁₆" hole into the cabinet about 1½" deep. Then rip walnut scraps to ¼" square. Whittle one end, paint with glue and hammer into the hole. Cut the peg flush* **(left).** *After pegging one side, fit the face frame into the front, glue the other side in place and clamp* **(right).**

Cove-Cutting

To cove-cut the moulding for the cabinet, first raise your table saw's blade to the depth you want to cove. Then clamp a straight piece of scrap to your table saw to the right outfeed side of your blade to use as a fence.

Set the angle of the fence by aligning your cove location from the board's edges with the infeed and outfeed tips of the saw blade. You should make the cove cut using several passes, increasing the blade height until finished (Photo A). Then set your blade angle to 45° and use the standard rip fence to cut the front detail (Photo B). Finally, put your fence on the left side of the blade and cut the details on the back using the same 45° setting (Photo C).

step 5 *The top crown is made with 4/4 maple; the coved piece below it is made from ³⁄₄" stock.*

step 6 *Here's what the door looks like before assembly. Note how the mortises for the rails are deeper than the grooves for the panel.*

in from the edge and ends in a ⅛" flat on the edge. To assemble the door, apply glue only to the mortise-and-tenon joints, allowing the panel to "float" without glue in the frame. Clamp the door and let dry, then peg the mortises using the same technique you used for the frame. The cockbeading around the door is made from ⅛" × ⁷⁄₁₆" scrap. Use a router to put a full roundover on one edge and then glue it on the frame around the door.

The Antique Touch

You could buy reproduction hinges and screws and spend a lot of money. Or you could try to make the hardware look old using highly diluted nitric acid, like many reproduction companies do. This can be dangerous to you and the environment. Or, even easier, you can do what I do and age your hardware with gun blue, which is available at most hardware stores. Gun blue is usually used on gun barrels to give the metal a blue look, but it works great on steel screws and hinges.

The door handle is made from a simple store-bought pull, a ⅛" dowel and a piece of scrap maple cut to the shape shown in step 7. Peen the dowel after gluing it into the scrap piece.

The antiqued 2" butt hinges were let into the door and frame about ¹⁄₁₆" on each side using a jig and router, though they could be hand cut with a chisel to carry the authentic technique even further. To finish, I sand the entire piece to either 180 or 220 grit. Then I brush on a water-based aniline dye, wipe off the excess and then sand with 400-grit sandpaper. Next I spray on a sealer and sand again with 320-grit sandpaper. Then I finish the entire piece with three or four coats of spray lacquer. Finally, I screw brass hangers to the back of the cabinet.

step 7 *This door knob and turn allows the cabinet to be latched by twisting.*

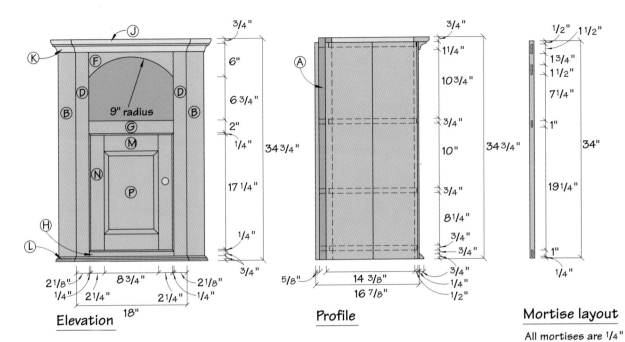

Elevation

3/4"
6"
6 3/4"
2"
1/4"
34 3/4"
17 1/4"
1/4"
3/4"

9" radius

2 1/8"
1/4"
2 1/4"
8 3/4"
2 1/4"
2 1/8"
1/4"
18"

Profile

3/4"
1 1/4"
10 3/4"
3/4"
10"
34 3/4"
3/4"
8 1/4"
3/4"
3/4"
3/4"
1/4"
1/2"

5/8"
14 3/8"
16 7/8"

Mortise layout

1/2"
1 1/2"
1 3/4"
1 1/2"
7 1/4"
1"
34"
19 1/4"
1"
1/4"

All mortises are 1/4"
wide and centered
on the stile.

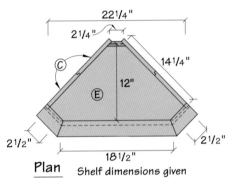

Plan   Shelf dimensions given

22 1/4"
2 1/4"
14 1/4"
12"
2 1/2"
2 1/2"
18 1/2"

Gun Blue Trick

To make your steel screws and hinges look authentic, soak them in gun blue for a few seconds, or until they turn black, and remove them.

Schedule of Materials: SHAKER HANGING CABINET

No.	Ltr.	Item	Dimensions T W L	Material
1	A	Back stile	3/4" x 2 3/4" x 34"	Maple
2	B	End stiles	3/4" x 4" x 34"	Maple
4	C	Back pieces	5/8" x 7 5/8" x 32"	Maple
2	D	Face stiles	3/4" x 2 1/8" x 34"	Maple
4	E	Shelves	3/4" x 12" x 22 1/4"	Maple
1	F	Curved face rail	3/4" x 6" x 15 3/4"*	Maple
1	G	Middle face rail	3/4" x 2" x 15 3/4"*	Maple
1	H	Bottom face rail	3/4" x 1 1/2" x 15 3/4"*	Maple
1	J	Top crown	3/4" x 2 1/2" x 31 1/2"	Maple
1	K	Crown moulding	3/4" x 2" x 31 1/2"	Maple
1	L	Bottom moulding	3/4" x 5/8" x 27 1/2"	Maple
Door				
2	M	Rails	3/4" x 2 1/4" x 10 1/2"*	Maple
2	N	Stiles	3/4" x 2 1/4" x 17 1/4"	Maple
1	P	Panel	11/16" x 9 3/8" x 13 3/8"	Maple
		Cockbeading	1/4" x 15/16"	Maple

*This measurement includes tenon lengths on both sides.

Build these traditional
tables with help from
a tool usually reserved
for carpenters:
the power planer.

QUEEN ANNE

QUEEN ANNE
SIDE
TABLES

As I get a little older, I get more sedentary. My wife says I'm just looking for more places to set a drink down. In that spirit, I decided to draw on my experience making period furniture to come up with a set of end tables for the living room — one with a poplar clover-shaped top, the other with a curly maple porringer top. These tables come from designs that are roughly 250 years old. This places them squarely in the country interpretation of the Queen Anne style.

According to Leigh Keno, a noted New York antiques dealer and a regular on PBS's popular *Antiques Roadshow*, the term *porringer* is merely a convenient way for antique dealers to classify this type of table and probably has nothing to do with the way the table was used originally. Using the English word *porridge* (oatmeal) as the root word, the term is likely no more than 150 years old. *Porringer* is used today to describe a small soup or cereal bowl with a handle. Antique dealers most likely tried to use the name to pass off the round oversized corners — which were no more than a decorative element — as the accessories of a small breakfast table. That said, porringers in good condition will fetch thousands of dollars these days due to their rarity.

Making Aprons

These tables were made with simple mortise-and-tenon construction. Start by cutting the apron parts according to the Schedule of Materials. Next cut the ⅜" by 4"-wide by ⅞"-long tenons on the ends of the aprons.

Making Pockets

The last thing to do on the aprons is to drill the pocket holes for attaching the base to the top. Do this on a drill press with a 1¼" Forstner bit. Use a shop-built jig (the diagram for this jig is on page 110) to hold the aprons in place for drilling.

Leg Blanks

Although the legs look complicated, they are not. The secret is an offset turning technique. First cut the blanks ⅛" longer than in the schedule. This gives you some room to work with when turning the pad on the end of the foot.

Use a straightedge to make an X from corner to corner on both ends of the blank. This will aid in finding the center as well as marking the offset. Now, on the bottom of the legs, determine which corner will face out. On the bottom of each leg, measure ¼" from the center to the corner opposite the outside corner. This is the offset for the leg. Remember, the farther away from the center you go, the thinner the ankle (the area just above the pad) will be. Going any farther than ¼" is dangerously close to having a leg pop off your lathe.

Mark a line completely around the blank 6" down from the top of the blank. To save time roughing the blank, lay out a 1½"-diameter circle on the bottom of the blank. Set your jointer to 45°. Using the circle as a guide, lower the infeed table to the point where you can take the corner off, leaving about ⅛" to the circle. Go slow and joint to within ¼" of the line where the turning starts. Now mount the blank in the

step 1 *Lay out the scrollwork on the bottom of the aprons using the patterns supplied on page 110. Glue the patterns to ¼" plywood, cut them out, trace the pattern on your aprons and cut them out on a band saw. Make relief cuts on the inside radii so you can scroll them out easier.*

step 2 *When drilling pocket holes, make sure that the bottom of the pocket is at least ⅞" from the top edge of the apron to prevent the screws from poking through.*

step 3 *To cut the corners, first mount a blank between centers with the top toward the drive center. Then use a saw to cut a small kerf on each corner at the line 6" from the top. Don't cut too far or you won't be able to remove the kerf. With a roughing gouge and a skew chisel, turn a cylindrical blank from the saw kerf to the foot. At this point use a skew chisel to cut a small rounding up on the square corners of the top (see diagram). Repeat on all the legs and you're ready to do the offset turning.*

lathe.

After mounting a blank between centers with the top toward the drive center, cut a small kerf at the line where the turning stops. Don't cut too far or you won't be able to remove the kerf. With a roughing gouge and a skew

chisel, turn a cylindrical blank from the saw kerf to the foot. At this point use a skew chisel to round the corners of the pummel, the square part of the leg, where it meets the turned portion. Repeat on all the legs and you're ready to do the offset turning.

step 4 *When you turn the lathe on, the leg's spinning creates a ghost image of what the finished leg will look like. Remove that "ghost" material with a roughing gouge. Stop at the second line that you drew earlier. Lay the gouge on its left side at the second line and slowly rotate the gouge clockwise as you go to the left. Go very slowly until you get the hang of how the wood reacts to the gouge.*

Turning the Offset

Before resetting the legs, measure up from the bottom ⅛" and from that mark another ⅝". Turn the lathe on and follow the marks around with a pencil. Take a parting tool and set it on its side. Cut a small incision at the ⅝" mark. This creates a shadow line from which to begin the offset turning. Set the lathe for its lowest speed and reset the tailstock so the leg center is mounted in the offset mark. This might look like an awkward setup, but as you remove material the leg will turn with more stability. Finish the straight part of the leg with a skew chisel and the ankle with a roughing gouge. Finally, turn the pad foot as shown in step 5. Now is the time to sand the legs. Start with 120-grit sandpaper and finish with 150 grit.

Now cut the ⅜" × ⅞" × 4" mortises in the legs, ⁵⁄₁₆" in from the edge and ½" down from the top. Be careful when marking the locations of your mortises to make sure the turned feet face out. You'll notice that the mortises meet slightly at their bottoms. Simply plane away a little of the tenon where they meet. Now glue the base together. Start by gluing the short ends together and then attaching them to the long aprons.

step 5 *The last thing to do on the legs is turning the pad on the foot. You do this last, as removing the foot material also removes the offset center. Reset the bottom of the leg into the original center and, using a parting tool, turn away this "extra" length until it's about ³⁄₈" diameter. This gives you some extra distance from the live center. Then using a small spindle gouge, turn the pad of the foot till it meets the ³⁄₈" diameter. Sand the pad the same as the leg and you're done turning.*

step 6 *When you've done all you can with a power planer, use chisels and planes to sculpt underneath and remove material down to the marked line.*

After the glue is dry, finish sand the entire base, then lay out the holes for the cherry pegs. Any dark hardwood will do for the pegs, but cherry sands smooth and the end grain stains a dark color. Drill a ¼" hole 1" deep. Follow suit with ³⁄₁₆" and ⅛" bits, creating a ta-

pered hole. After shaping 16 square pegs (tapered on four sides to a point), tap one in until you feel and hear it seat. The sound of the hammer hitting the peg makes a distinctly different sound when it seats. No glue is required for this as you are running a peg

▮ supplies

Groff and Groff Lumber
(800) 342-0001
• **Curly maple**

Woodworker's Supply
(800) 645-9292
• **J.E. Moser's Golden Amber**
  Maple aniline dye

Garrett Wade
(800) 221-2942
www.garrettwade.com
• **Button-Lac shellac flakes,**
  #99P23.01, $19.95
• **Shellac solvent, #99P25.01,**
  $6.30 per quart

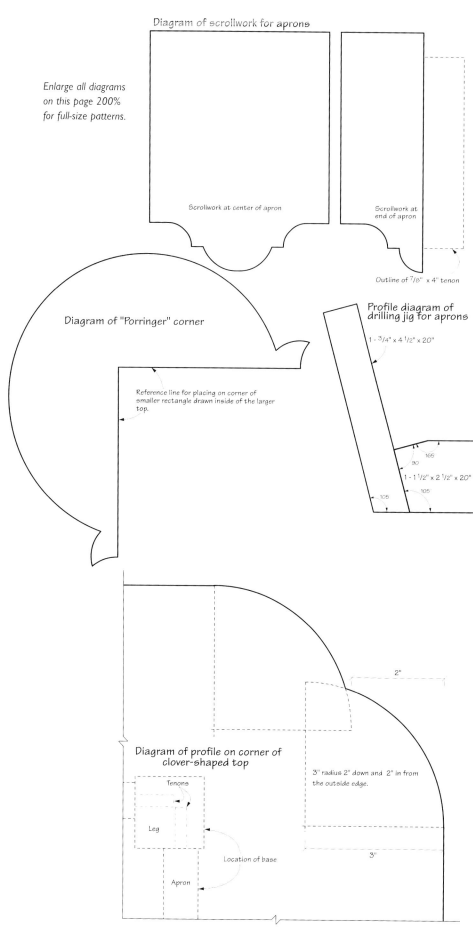

Diagram of scrollwork for aprons

Enlarge all diagrams on this page 200% for full-size patterns.

Scrollwork at center of apron

Scrollwork at end of apron

Outline of 7/8" x 4" tenon

Diagram of "Porringer" corner

Reference line for placing on corner of smaller rectangle drawn inside of the larger top.

Profile diagram of drilling jig for aprons

1 - 3/4" x 4 1/2" x 20"

165
90
105
105

1 - 1 1/2" x 2 1/2" x 20"

Diagram of profile on corner of clover-shaped top

Tenons

Leg

Apron

Location of base

2"

3" radius 2" down and 2" in from the outside edge.

3"

completely through the leg. It won't be coming out anytime soon. Cut the pegs, leaving 1/2" showing and sand until it is a rounded-over bump. Drill 1/4" holes into the pockets from the top of the base for attaching the top.

Make and Attach the Top

The top is the easiest part, but it can make or break the whole project. Wood selection is key. One hundred years ago, you could get extremely wide, highly figured curly maple at a low price. Amazingly most old porringers were one- or two-board tops. That's clear-figured wood 10" to 20" wide! Regrettably, those days are gone, and you will have to make do with the painfully high priced, narrow lumber you get today.

Poplar is easy to get in a decent width and length, but I had to try the Amish sawmills in eastern Pennsylvania to find a retail source for decent curly maple (see the Supplies box on page 109 for one such mill). I managed to find decent 4/4 that's about 7" wide and a nice piece of 8/4 for the legs. I wasn't sure how thick the legs would be when I started, so you could probably get away with 6/4 for leg stock.

The tops for both types of tables are the same size. They just require a different edge pattern. See diagram at left for the shape of each top. For the porringer top, lay out a 15¼" x 25¼" rectangle in the center of the top. Make a pattern for the top with ¼" plywood as you did with the aprons. When you lay the inside corner of the pattern over the outside corner of the drawn rectangle, the outside of the radius should just touch the edge of the top. Trace the pattern on all four corners and jigsaw the top out. For the clover-shaped top, things are easier. Make a pattern from the diagram supplied at left and trace the double radius on all four corners.

When you are done cutting out the shape of the top, chamfer the edges. Chamfering the edges lightens the overall look of the table, and the chisel

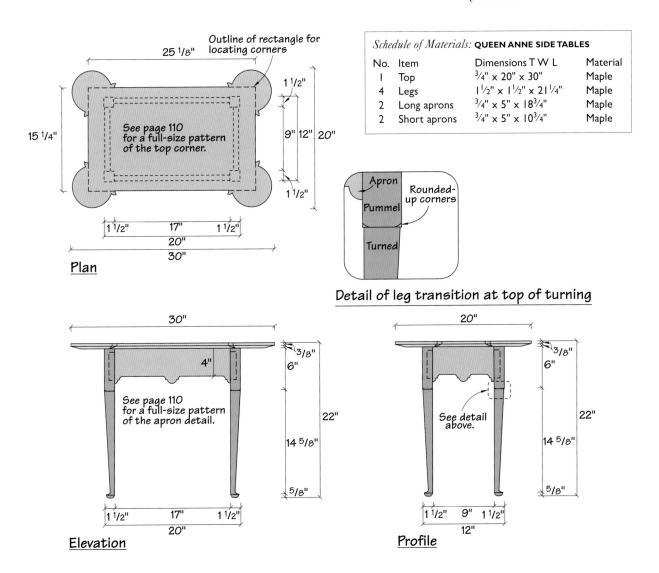

Schedule of Materials: QUEEN ANNE SIDE TABLES

No.	Item	Dimensions T W L	Material
1	Top	$^{3}/_{4}$" x 20" x 30"	Maple
4	Legs	$1^{1}/_{2}$" x $1^{1}/_{2}$" x $21^{1}/_{4}$"	Maple
2	Long aprons	$^{3}/_{4}$" x 5" x $18^{3}/_{4}$"	Maple
2	Short aprons	$^{3}/_{4}$" x 5" x $10^{3}/_{4}$"	Maple

Outline of rectangle for locating corners

See page 110 for a full-size pattern of the top corner.

Plan

Apron

Pummel

Turned

Rounded-up corners

Detail of leg transition at top of turning

See page 110 for a full-size pattern of the apron detail.

Elevation

See detail above.

Profile

work underneath has a very sculptural feel. Before chamfering, use a marking gauge to mark a line that is half the thickness of the top on the entire outside edge of the top. Next, use an adjustable square to mark a line around the underside of the top. For the porringer the measurement is 1½" and for the clover use a 2¼" line.

I chamfered the edges with a power planer. It's a tool used mostly by carpenters to remove material from doors when fitting and installing them. And in that role, this tool is unequaled. Finish sand the top to 150 grit.

The last assembly chore is to screw the top to the base. Begin by laying the top upside down on a blanket. Center the base on the top and screw it down with no. 10 × 1½" wood screws.

How Thick Is It Anyway?

When lumberyards count up the board footage that you buy, it's referred to as a tally. The "tallyman" carries a special notebook and a strange floppy stick called a "tallystick" (go figure!) with odd measurements on it. The lumber you buy is sorted by how many quarters of an inch thick it is. This system starts at 4/4 for 1" thickness on up to 16/4 for 4" lumber.

In finishing the clover table, I sprayed on a custom-mixed aniline dye followed by three coats of clear finish. This turned the poplar to a mahogany-like color.

The porringer was a different story. To begin finishing, I hand-scraped the top with a Stanley #80 cabinet scraper.

With the lack of abrasive sandpaper 250 years ago, this is how the old tables were made ready to finish. Scraping with a properly prepared scraper blade will show up as rows of slight depressions (¹⁄₃₂" deep) with ridges about 2½" apart. I stained the wood with aniline dye, then applied one coat of boiled linseed oil and finished the table with four coats of dark shellac. This imparts a nice honey brown color to the curly maple and is easy to repair. Now where did I put that drink?

Discover what it was
like to work wood
200 years ago when
all you had were a
few well-tuned saws,
a couple chisels and
a steady hand.

SHAKER
STEP STOOL

Back when the Shakers started making furniture in the late 18th century, the only tools available to them were powered by people. No table saws, no electric jointers or planers. Your tool kit consisted largely of handsaws, chisels and planes. Your planer, jointer and table saw were usually a young apprentice who prepared stock by hand. The skilled woodworkers handled most joinery tasks.

Shakers eagerly sought out power tools and technology to help them do their work. But during the heyday of most Shaker communities, hand tools did most of the work.

Today there is a group of woodworkers who still pride themselves in building furniture this way. They call themselves "Neanderthals." And the way they communicate is, ironically, usually through the Internet. We thought it would be interesting to build a project using only hand tools to get a feel for how early Shakers and electronic-age Neanderthals work. Admittedly, we copped out on one aspect of this project: We didn't surface the lumber from rough stock using hand tools. We rationalized this by figuring an apprentice would have done this work.

I think you'll enjoy unplugging your router for a few days to tackle this modest but satisfying project. And if you cannot give up your power tools, you can rest easy knowing that the early Shakers would have paid almost any price for that precision plunge router on your bench.

These stools were used in Shaker housing to get to the upper drawers in the enormous chests built for communal use. The stool was placed against the lower part of a chest for support. If you want to use this as a freestanding

The 10-Cent Dovetail Jig

In the midst of laying out the dovetails for these stools, I decided I wanted a way to make the cuts for my tails as clean, accurate and quick as possible. There are 44 angled cuts for the dovetails alone. So I made this jig, and I think it will help the first-timers out there. Look at this jig as training wheels for cutting tails.

Basically, the jig is an 'H' that fits over your work and guides your saw at the perfect angle. Flip the jig over, and it cuts the other way. Tails have never been easier to do. Begin by cutting two side pieces $1/2$" x 3" x 4" from plywood. Then cut the spacer that goes between the two using falloff from your stool. This will ensure your jig sleeves tightly over your work. The spacer should be $3/4$" x $3/8$" x 4". I glued and nailed the spacer between the two sides and then cut one end at a 7° or 9° angle. I cheated and used a chop saw for this cut.

Then cut a face piece ($1/2$" x 3" x 5") out of plywood. Glue and nail the face on the angled ends of the H. Now use a ryoba saw and a coping saw to cut the notches out of the face and fit the jig to your dovetailing stock with a rasp. When you've got a snug fit, try a couple of test cuts. Gently hold the ryoba saw against the jig as you begin to make your cut. The guide will do the rest of the work.

It's pretty easy to hold the blade in position and cut down to the gauge marks. As a bonus, you can use the other end of the jig to make square cuts. With practice, you won't even have to trim the tails when fitting.

Clamp a straightedge to the back line of the stool, gently press the saw against it and rip the back edge. Use the ripping teeth on the back of the ryoba saw.

After cutting the bottom, lay out the radius.

stool, add a hand rail.

The tools needed are as follows: clamps, a block plane, a jack plane, a couple Japanese saws, two sharp chisels, a coping saw and a hand drill. For marking dovetails, I use a sharp knife, a square and a sliding T-bevel.

Begin construction by laying out the panels for the sides. Use a cardboard template to lay out the best yield from your panels. Because you aren't going to make these cuts with a table saw, you will have to make stopped crosscuts and rips in the middle of the panels to cut out the steps using handsaws. I've found the best way to do this is with Japanese saws.

Courtesy of Japan

There is a style of saw called an azebi-ki-nokogiri. In short, it's a saw with a curved blade for doing a "plunge" cut in the middle of a panel. The other saw

After laying out the steps, start making the plunge cuts in the panel for each rise and run on the steps. Remember to use the larger ripping teeth for the long grain and the shorter crosscutting teeth for the cross-grain. Start each cut by gently pressing the saw against the straightedge and use a rocking motion to use the entire length of the blade to make the cut.

When you've penetrated the other side of the panel, cut a slot large enough for the ryoba saw. Finish the cuts into the inside and outside corners, but be sure to use the correct teeth for the direction you are cutting.

I used was a ryoba saw. It's a two-edged blade with rip teeth on one edge and crosscut teeth on the other. There are other Japanese saws designed for dovetailing, but I appreciate the utility of the two-sided blade.

Begin by laying out your cutting lines in pencil on the sides. The object is to first cut the back edge of the side, then cut the bottom edge square to that. Then lay out the steps from these two perpendicular lines.

Cutting a straight line isn't difficult, especially if you clamp a piece of wood to your work to serve as a guide. Simply clamp the guide to the work and begin making the cut with your ryoba saw. Use your fingers to gently hold the blade against your guide. Take it slowly and your cut will be true.

Set up another straightedge and, using the finer crosscut teeth of the ryoba saw, cut in about 4" from the front and back edges of the stool. Mark the center of the bottom and lay out a 9"-diameter semicircle. Now cut the half circle on the sides, using a com-

The results speak for themselves. With a kerf less than $1/16$", it's possible to do some fine cutting. Notice the radiused cuts that resemble cuts from a table saw. These marks are from the azebiki-noko-giri saw.

After cleaning up the edges of the side panels, begin laying out the tails on the treads. Use the diagram to help. If you're going to use the training-wheels jig described in the sidebar "The 10-Cent Dovetail Jig," don't lay out the sides of the tails on the top and bottom of the tread. Simply lay out the $1/8$" spaces between the tails on the ends. Use the jig to define the tail shape. Braver souls will start with a marking gauge and then, using a sliding T-bevel set to 7°, make knife cuts into the wood to mark the tails. If you can't see the cut lines, use a sharp pencil to put a little "makeup" on them.

Dovetail layout detail

Tread

3/4"

1" | 1 7/16" | 1 7/16" | 1"
1/8" | 1/8" | 1/8"
5 1/4"

1/4"
1 3/4"
1/4"

Back brace | Tread brace | 2"
1/4"

3/4" | 3/4"

7° angle on tails for hardwood (shown)
9° angle for softwoods

No.	Ltr.	Item	Dimensions T W L	Material
		Schedule of Materials: **SHAKER STEP STOOL**		
2	A	Sides	¾" × 15¾" × 25½"	Walnut
3	B	Treads	¾" × 5¼" × 16"	Walnut
5	C	Braces	¾" × 2¼" × 16"	Walnut

Back brace gets two-sided tail.

C

B

A

5 1/4" | 5 1/4" | 5 1/4"
3/4" | 3/4" | 3/4"
3/4" | 3 3/4" | 4 1/2" | 4 1/2"

3/4"
2"
1/4"

6 1/4"

See detail for dovetail layout.

1/4"
1 3/4"
1/4"

14"

3/4"
2"
1/4"
5 1/2"

3/4"
2"
1/4"
5 1/2"

3/4"
2"
1/4"
5 1/2"

8 1/2"

8 1/2"

8 1/2"

25 1/2"

4 1/2" radius

3 3/8" | 9" | 3 3/8"
15 3/4"

Those of you using the training-wheels jig can now cut all of the tails on the treads and braces. You'll have to figure out which way the jig works best on each cut. If you're not sure, mark the tails with a pencil so there's no confusion. I like to use the rip side of the ryoba saw to cut dovetails. This might rankle some of the hardcore Neanderthals out there, but I've found it's aggressive and the cut needs little or no trimming after.

pass saw. Clean up your cuts with sandpaper.

The best way to cut the steps is to make a plunge cut with the azebiki saw and finish with the ryoba saw, crosscutting against the grain and ripping with the grain. Again, clamping a piece of straight wood to your work will ensure your cuts are straight.

There's nothing fast about this process. Slow and deliberate will do the trick. Once the sides are complete, cut the treads and risers to size. Clean them up with a plane and make sure everything's square.

Dovetails

Start cutting the dovetail joints by laying out the tails on the treads and risers according to the diagram. On hardwood joints, the dovetail angles should be at a 1:8 ratio (7°). On softwoods the ratio is

Clamp a panel into a vise and use the tails on the tread ends and braces to mark the locations for the pins and brace notches. Use a knife to get a more accurate layout. Since they're easier to fit, I don't use a jig for the pins. Just lay them out from the tail marks, using a knife and sliding T-bevel set to 7°. Fit the pins to the tails with a four-in-hand rasp, removing material from the pins until the tread can be lightly tapped onto the side. Use a backer block to do this so you don't split the tread.

After defining the tails, remove the little triangle of wood between them with a coping saw. The $1/8$" gap is big enough for a small chisel to fit into for trimming.

1:6 (9°). Cut the tails, then number each joint for reference.

I built a couple little jigs to make cutting my tails easier. See the accompanying sidebar, "The 10-Cent Dovetail Jig," for details.

Now use the tails to lay out the pins on the side pieces. Cut the tails by making the first cuts with the ryoba saw and clean out the waste with a coping saw. Now try to fit the joints. If they are too tight, use a chisel to clean up the joint. If they are too loose, you can glue thin shavings into the joint to fill it out. Most people will never notice.

When cut correctly, the joints should tap together and be snug without beating on the stool. When you're satisfied with the fit, glue all the joints and mating edges together. Sand and apply three coats of your favorite finish. I used Watco, an oil and varnish blend.

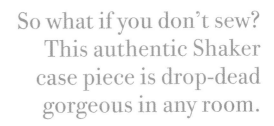

So what if you don't sew? This authentic Shaker case piece is drop-dead gorgeous in any room.

SHAKER

TAILOR'S CABINET

This tailor's cabinet was brought to my attention by a customer who wanted one just like it. She had seen the piece in John Kassay's *The Book of Shaker Furniture*. The original was made in Watervliet, New York, during the first half of the 19th century, using plain and figured maple, and pine for the panels and interior pieces. The book also describes the drop-leaf on the original as being of walnut, indicating it may have been added later. My customer wasn't looking for a walnut leaf or pine sides, and I assured her I could make those changes.

This is a great storage piece for any number of rooms in the house, and while the leaf adds character, it doesn't add all that much space. Even though the leaf may never be used, I like the way it looks; so it's well worth the effort.

The basic construction of the cabinet is frame and loose panel for the sides and back. The front is a mortised-and-tenoned frame filled with drawers. Construction starts with the legs. Cut them to size according to the Schedule of Materials, then mark the foot of each leg for the simple tapered turning. The taper starts 4⅞" from the bottom. At the top of the taper the leg is turned from a 1⅝" square post to a 1½" round, then tapered to 1" at the base.

With all four legs tapered, determine the arrangement of the legs to show off the best figure and mark them to keep them straight. The sides and back of the cabinet are made of panels and rails with tenons that fit into grooves that are cut on the inside faces of the legs. The grooves are ⅜"-wide by 1⅛"-deep and are run ¼" in from the outside edge of the leg. I used a router table to run the grooves, lowering the leg onto the bit to start the cut and lifting at the end of the cut. Use indexing marks on the router table fence to indicate when to start and stop the groove. Make the same groove in the side and back rails and stiles to hold the panels in place. The groove will be off-center on the rails, so determine which face is most attractive and run the grooves with the best side on the ¼" offset while the router table is set up.

The next step is to cut the mortises in the legs, then form the tenons on the front rails. You'll see in the photo that the front rails have double tenons for extra strength. Mark the mortise locations on the front legs, then use a mortiser or router to cut the mortises. While using the mortiser, mark the locations for the 10 drawer runners on the inside of the face rails and cut those mortises, as well. Then set your table saw to cut the double tenons on the ends of the front rails.

With the tenons and mortises formed, and the legs turned, the puzzle begins to take shape when you glue up the front frame. Notice the double-tenon used in the legs for extra strength.

It never hurts to check the fit when so many pieces come together in one place. Check the spacing of the panels and rails into the legs and adjust as necessary.

The front stile dividing the upper four drawers is attached to the second rail with a half-lap or bridle joint, cut exactly in the center of the rail and the stile. I made these cuts on the table saw, nibbling away with repeated passes. Assemble the front frame by starting with the stile, attaching it to the top and third rails using pegs through the rails.

Next cut the tenons on the ends of the side and back rails and back stiles. I again used the table saw to make these cuts. The tenons are centered on the pieces and offset from the center to match the grooves.

Cut rabbets on all four sides of the side and back panels. As these are ½"-thick pieces, a ¼" rabbet forms the tenon easily so that the inside faces of the panels and the rails will be flush on the inside. By setting your table saw's rip fence to ¼" (with the blade set at ¼" high) the rabbets can be easily cut on the saw by running the panels on end.

To add a nice detail to the piece, put a beading bit in your router and run a ¼" detail on both edges of the side center rail and on the inside edges of the top and bottom rails. Cut the notches for the drop leaf support in the top

With everything sitting in place, it's time to add the back and clamp everything down. Notice the two drawer support rails attached to the back.

back rail according to the diagram, then assemble the back and rear legs. Use glue on the rail and stile tenons, but don't glue the panels, so the wood can move.

Drawer Supports

While the glue is drying, turn to the drawer supports. There are four side supports and two center supports for the upper drawers, and four side sup-

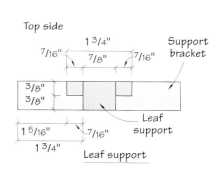

Leaf support

Schedule of Materials: **SHAKER TAILOR'S CABINET**

No.	Item	Dimensions T W L	Wood	Notes*
4	Legs	1 5/8" x 1 5/8" x 30 1/2"	P	
4	Side rails, top/bot.	3/4" x 2 1/2" x 20 3/4"	P	1" TBE
2	Side rails, middle	3/4" x 2 3/4" x 20 3/4"	P	1" TBE
2	Back rails, top/bot.	3/4" x 2 1/2" x 33 7/8"	P	1" TBE
1	Back rail, middle	3/4" x 2 3/4" x 33 7/8"	P	1" TBE
2	Back stiles	3/4" x 2 3/4" x 10 13/16"	P	1" TBE
5	Front rails	7/8" x 1 5/8" x 33 7/8"	P	1" TBE
1	Front stile	7/8" x 1 5/8" x 10 3/8"	P	Half-lap
4	End panels	1/2" x 9 3/8" x 19 3/8"	P	3/8" TAS
4	Back panels	1/2" x 9 3/8" x 15 3/16"	P	3/8" TAS
4	Drawer runners	3/4" x 2 1/8" x 18 7/8"	S	3/8" TOE
2	Drawer supports	3/4" x 1 5/8" x 33 1/8"	S	
4	Drawer runners	3/4" x 2 1/8" x 18 7/8"	S	3/8"/1" T
2	Drawer runners	3/4" x 3" x 18 7/8"	S	3/8"/1" T
8	Drawer sides	1/2" x 4 1/2" x 19"	S	
4	Drawer backs	1/2" x 3 3/4" x 15 3/8"	S	
4	Drawer fronts	7/8" x 5" x 16 1/8"	P	3/8" lip 3X
4	Drawer bottoms	5/8" x 16" x 19 1/4"	S	CTF
4	Drawer sides	1/2" x 5 1/2" x 19"	S	
2	Drawer backs	1/2" x 4 3/4" x 31 3/4"	S	
2	Drawer fronts	7/8" x 6" x 32 3/8"	P	3/8" lip 3X
2	Drawer bottoms	5/8" x 32" x 19 1/4"	S	CTF
1	Top	3/4" x 24" x 45 1/8"	P	
1	Leaf	3/4" x 6 3/4" x 45 1/8"	P	
4	Support brackets	3/4" x 1 3/4" x 19 3/16"	S	
2	Leaf supports	3/4" x 1 3/4" x 21"	S	
10	Drawer guides	3/4" x 7/8" x 16"	S	

*TBE = tenon both ends TAS = tenon all sides TOE = tenon one end CTF = cut to fit

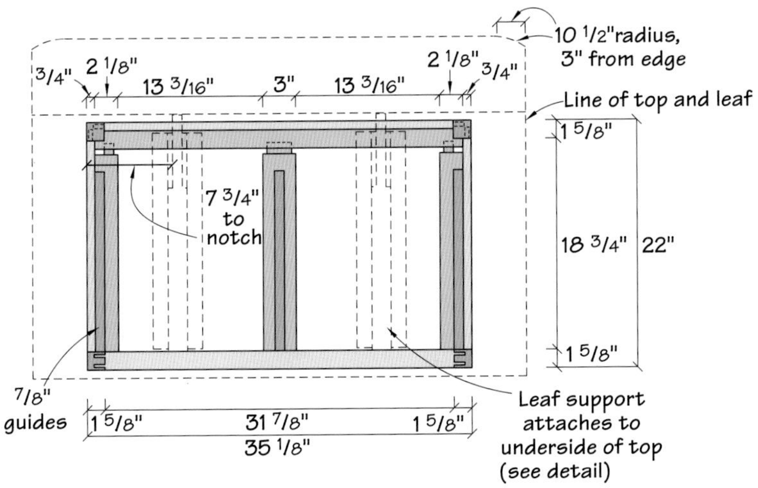

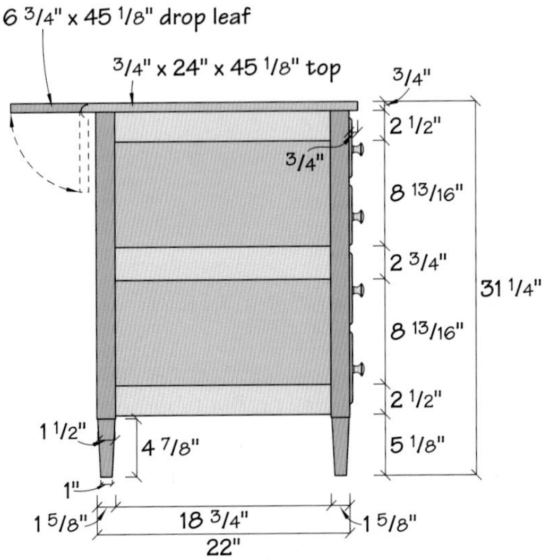

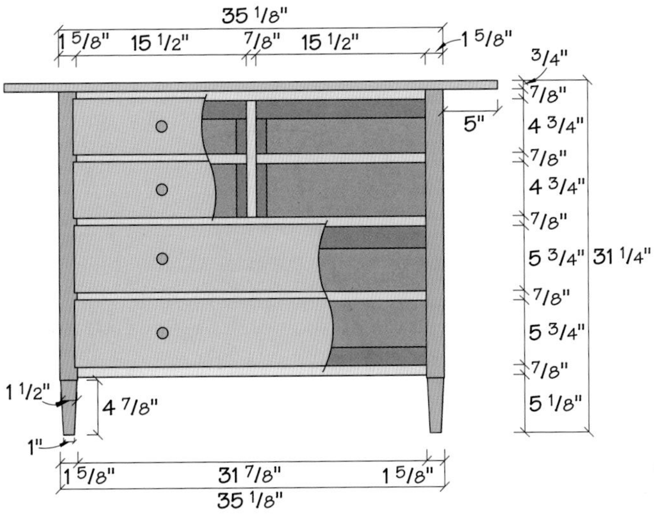

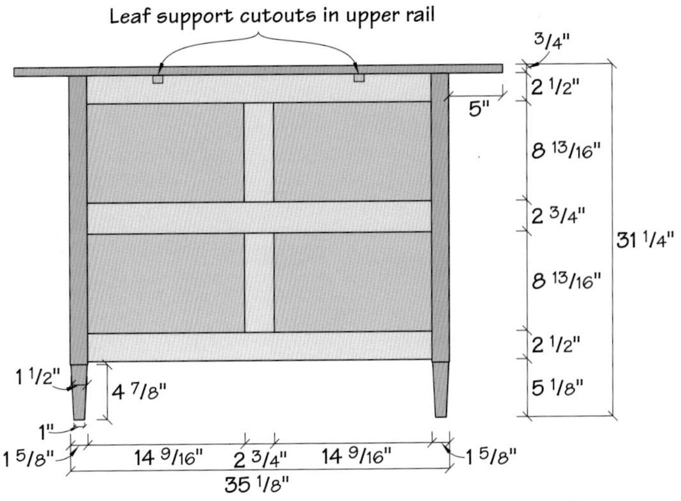

Making a Rule Joint

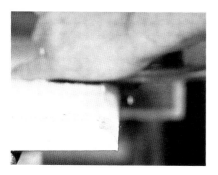

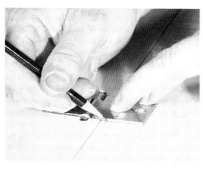

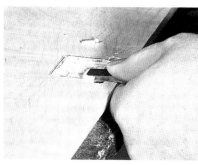

The rule joint for the top and leaf attachment requires a certain amount of accuracy, but it pays off in the end. With a little care, a test piece isn't even necessary. I used a CMT ½" cove bit (#837.850.11, $38.90 suggested retail) and a CMT ½" roundover bit (#838.880.11, $40.50 suggested retail). Call CMT, (888) 268-2487 for a dealer in your area. You can find sets in other catalogs.

The first step is to run the roundover bit on the top piece, leaving about a ⅛" shoulder at the top.

Use the cove bit to run the profile on the leaf, making the cut less deep than should be necessary. Place the two pieces together to check the fit; adjust the depth of the cove cut deeper until the top surfaces are flush.

Next, turn the top and leaf over and mark the locations for the hinges so that the center of the barrel is ½" from the lip of the top. With the location marked, use a ⁵⁄₁₆" straight bit to make a relief cut in the underside of the top piece that's deep enough for the barrel of the hinge to slip into. Allow for the thickness of the hinge leaf when determining the depth of the recess.

With the barrel recessed into the top, mark the hinge location on the top and leaf, and rout a recess for the hinge leaves into both pieces. The same bit used to rout in the barrel should work for this operation, as well.

When you rout for the hinge leaf recess, make the cuts short of the pencil line, then use a chisel to clean up the recess. Start the cleanup by defining the perimeter of the recess using a chisel. Pare the material at the pencil marks. Then use the chisel held flat to remove the waste. Now simply attach the hinges, mark the length of the top and cut the top and leaf to length.

To guide the drawers smoothly, I attach simple poplar strips with a brad nailer to the drawer supports. A little wax on the supports, and the drawer runs smooth as silk.

ports for the lower drawers.

Cut the supports to the sizes given in the Schedule of Materials. The supports are all a little different, but let's start with the front end. Make ¾" × 1¾" × ¾"-long tenons on the front of all the side supports. Make ¾" × 2" × ¾"-long tenons on the front of the two center supports. Only the six top supports have tenons on the back end. Make the side support tenons ¾" × 1¾" × 1" long, and the two center supports ¾" × 2" × 1" long. The four lower drawer supports are notched ¾" × 1" around the the rear leg, and then tapered on the inside edge. These are then nailed in place, with reproduction nails, to the rear leg after assembly.

To attach the upper drawer supports at the rear of the cabinet, mortise and then nail two support battens in place on the back legs.

You're now ready to assemble. Test fit the side panels and rails in the back legs, and check the fit of the front frame to the sides. If everything fits well, lay the face frame on your work surface and glue the side rails to the front legs (again leaving the panels glue-free) then glue the drawer supports into their mortises in the front frame. Lower the back into place, leaving the tenons on the drawer supports glue-free. Check for square and clamp

The three-piece leaf supports are kind of clever. By trapping the support itself between the front and back of the case, the support has a built-in stop in both the open and closed position.

The drawers are constructed using dovetails (half-blind on the front and through at the back) and a beveled bottom slipped into grooves in the front and sides.

A trick from our clever ancestors was to cut a slot in the back edge of the solid wood bottom and nail the bottom in place at the slot, with the bottom glued to the front. This allows the bottom to move with changes in humidity.

the cabinet until the glue is dry.

The drawer supports provide support for the bottom of the drawers, but to get them to move well they also need some guides to control side-to-side movement. These ¾" × ⅞"-wide strips are simply tacked in place to the drawer supports to guide the drawer sides.

While you're still working on the inside of the cabinet, cut the leaf supports and the four brackets to support them to size. Each pair of brackets is rabbeted ⅜" × ⁷⁄₁₆" on one side, and the leaf supports are rabbeted on both sides to form a stubby T cross-section. Then notch the support as shown in the photo and chamfer or round the end to avoid sharp corners. Later you will screw the brackets to the underside of the top with the arm protruding through the notches you cut in the back rail.

Drawers and Details

The drawers are of standard construction (by 19th-century standards, that is) with hand-cut dovetails and a solid wood bottom. Cut a ⅜" × ½" rabbet on three sides of the drawer fronts, then use the same beading detail as on the side rails to dress up all four edges of each drawer.

It's now time to get to the rule joint

that attaches the drop-leaf to the top. First glue up the large top, leaving it oversized for length until after the top and leaf have been attached by the hinges so the lengths will match perfectly. Use the information in the sidebar, "Making a Rule Joint," to cut the rule joint. I use standard hinges for my drop-leaf. If you purchase special drop-leaf hinges, then you won't have to rout a recess for the barrel as shown.

The top is attached to the cabinet by using rectangular wooden "buttons" that have a short tongue. The tongue slips into grooves cut in the side rails with a router and a slot cutter. If you don't feel like making your own but-

tons, you can purchase metal clips through most hardware catalogs. Cut the slots wide enough to allow the top room for wood movement. Attach the leaf supports to the top at this time.

After a good sanding, the cabinet is ready to finish. If you've read any of my earlier pieces in *Popular Woodworking* magazine, you may have noticed I have a favorite finish for curly maple furniture. I used that finish again on this piece — J.E. Moser's Golden Amber Maple, a water-based aniline dye. After the dye is dry, lightly sand the entire piece to remove any raised grain, then top coat the piece with lacquer or your favorite protective finish.

If you've never built a
face frame cabinet, learn
the tricks that ensure a
square-looking case,
tight joints and doors
that work as you build
this small cabinet.

MEDICINE CABINET

I've built hundreds of single-door cabinets like this one. Some people use them as spice cabinets. Others use them in the bathroom as a medicine cabinet. As I was building this particular cabinet, it occurred to me that it would be an excellent project for beginners. It has all the traditional components of larger-scale cabinetry, yet it doesn't need a lot of material or tooling. Once you've built this cabinet, you can build something bigger using the same principles. Intermediate woodworkers might also pick up a trick or two because I build my cabinets just a bit differently.

Choose Your Wood

I used tiger maple for this project, but if this is your first cabinet, you might want to use poplar and then paint the finished item. Poplar is easy to work with and less expensive than maple, especially if the maple has some figure.

As in larger cabinets, most of the major components are made from ¾"-thick stock: the case sides, top, bottom, plus the rails and stiles for the door and the face frame. This cabinet has a solid-wood shiplapped back that's made from ½"-thick pieces; the door panel is ⅝" thick.

Face Frame: The Place to Start

It seems logical to begin by constructing the case. Don't. The size of your case and door are all determined by your face frame. Build it first and then you'll use your face frame to lay out your case and door. All face frames are made up of rails and stiles, much like a door. The stiles are the vertical pieces. The rails are the horizontal pieces that go between the stiles.

When you rip your stiles to width on your table saw, make the rip ¹⁄₁₆" wider than stated on the Schedule of Materials. You need this extra to overhang the sides of your case so you can trim it flush with a flush-cutting bit in a router. Once your pieces are cut to size, join the rails and stiles using mortise-and-tenon joints.

Begin by cutting the tenons on the rail ends. I know the books say to cut the mortise first, but I've found it's easier to lay out your mortises after your tenons are cut. Try it, and I think you'll agree.

The tenons should be ⅜" thick (one-half as thick as your stock), centered on the rail and 1" long. I cut ½" shoulders on the tenons. If they're any smaller, the mortise might blow out. Now use your tenons to lay out your mortises on the stiles. Hold the tenon flat against the edge where the mortise will go and use the tenon like a ruler to mark your mortise.

Now cut your mortises. Make them all ¹¹⁄₁₆" deep, which will prevent your

Adding this beaded moulding to the inside of the face frame creates a nice shadow line around the door. Miter, glue and nail it in place. Don't forget to putty your nail holes.

Fit your door in the face frame before you attach the face frame to the case. Everything lays flat on your bench as you work. You'll find this procedure is a faster and easier way to get perfect results.

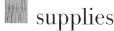 **supplies**

Rockler, (800) 279-4441
www.rockler.com
• **hinges for door, #31495, $5.99/pair**

Horton Brasses Inc.
(800) 754-9127
www.horton-brasses.com
• **machine screw fitting, #K-12 w/MSF, call for pricing**

1"-long tenons from bottoming out. You don't want your tenons to wobble in your mortises, yet you don't want to have to beat the tenon in place.

Dry fit your face frame, then put glue on the mortise walls and clamp it up. While you're waiting for it to dry, turn your attention to the bead moulding that goes on the inside edge of the face frames.

Years ago, I used to cut the beading into the rails and stiles. Then I would have to miter the bead and cut away the beading where the rails and stiles were joined. It sounds like a pain, and it was. Now I simply make my bead moulding separate from my face frame and miter, nail and glue it in place. It looks just as good.

To make the bead moulding, put a ¼" beading bit in your router and mount it in a router table. Then take a ¾"-thick board that's about 4" wide and cut the bead on one edge. Take that board to your table saw, set your rip fence to make a ¾"-wide cut and rip the bead from the wide board. Repeat this process three more times.

Now take your strips and run them through your planer to reduce them in thickness to ⁷⁄₁₆". Miter the corners; then glue and nail them in place. Sand both sides of your face frame with 100-grit sandpaper and move on to building the door.

The Door

Why make the door next? Well, for one thing, it is easier to hang your door in

Schedule of Materials: TIGER MAPLE MEDICINE CABINET

No.	Item	Dimensions T W L
2	Face frame stiles	¾" x 2¼" x 30"
1	Top face frame rail	¾" x 2⅞" x 15½"
1	Bottom face frame rail	¾" x 1½" x 15½"
2	Door stiles	¾" x 2½" x 25"
1	Top door rail	¾" x 2½" x 9⅞"
1	Bottom door rail	¾" x 3½" x 9⅞"
1	Door panel	⅝" x 8⅜" x 19½"
2	Case sides	¾" x 6" x 30"
2	Top & Bottom	¾" x 5½" x 17"
4	Shelves	¾" x 5⁷⁄₁₆" x 16⁷⁄₁₆"
	Back boards*	½" x 17" x 30"
	Top moulding	¾" x 2" x 36"

*Use any number of random-width boards to create the back, totalling 17" in width.

your face frame before you nail the face frame to your case.

I build my doors so they are the same size as my opening, then I shave off a little so there's a ¹⁄₁₆" gap all around. This way if the door or face frame is out of square, I can taper the door edges to fit, hiding my error.

The door is built much like the face frame, using the same size mortises and tenons. The biggest difference is that you will need to cut a groove in your rails and stiles for the door panel, so your tenons must be haunched. A *haunch* is a little extra width in the tenon's shoulder that fills in the groove on the end of the stile.

Begin by cutting a ¾"-deep by ¼"-wide groove down the center of one long edge of your rails and stiles. Cut your tenons on your rails. Then cut your mortises on your stiles. Dry fit the

pieces together and measure how big the center panel should be.

You want the panel to float to allow seasonal expansion and contraction, so cut the panel to allow ⅛" expansion on either side. Now raise the door panel using your table saw or a cutter in your router table. Practice on scrap pieces of ⅝" stock so you achieve the right lip, angle and fit.

When the panel is complete, sand the raised section, then glue up the door. Be careful not to get any glue in the groove that holds the panel. When the glue is dry, hang the door in your face frame.

Finally, the Case

The case is simple. The top and bottom pieces fit into ¼"-deep dadoes and rabbets on the sides. The back rests in a rabbet on the sides and is nailed to the back edge of the top and bottom pieces.

You'll use your face frame to lay out your joints on the sides. You want the bottom piece to end up ¹⁄₁₆" higher than the top edge of the bottom rail on your face frame. This allows your bottom to act as a stop for the door. Mark the location of that ¼"-deep dado and cut.

The top piece rests in a ¼"-deep by ¾"-wide rabbet on the sides. Cut that using your table saw. Then cut the ½"-deep by ¼"-wide rabbet on the back edge of the sides.

Drill holes for shelf pins and space them 1" apart on the sides. Sand the inside of the case. You'll notice that the top and bottom are ½" narrower than the sides. This is to give you a good place to nail the back pieces to the case. Assemble the case using glue and nails, making sure the top, bottom and sides are all flush at the front.

Attach the face frame to the case using glue and nails. Trim the face frame flush to the case using a bearing-guided flush-cutting bit in your router. Finish sand the cabinet to 180 grit.

Take your scrap pieces and use them to make a shiplapped back. Cut a ¼" × ½" rabbet on the edges and then cut a bead on one edge using a ¼" beading bit in your router table. You want to give the back pieces room to expand and contract, about ⅛" between each board should be fine.

Cut the moulding for the top so it resembles the drawing detail below. Finish sand everything, then nail the moulding to the top.

I like to peg the tenons in my doors to add a little strength. Drill a ¼"-diameter hole most of the way through the stile and tenon. Then whittle a square piece of stock so it's round on one end, put glue in the hole and pound it in place. Cut the peg nearly flush. You want it to be a little proud of the stile — it's a traditional touch.

Break all the edges of the case with 120-grit sandpaper, and putty all your nail holes. Paint, dye or stain all the components. I used a water-based aniline dye. Then add two coats of clear finish and nail the back pieces in place. Hang the cabinet by screwing through the back boards into a stud in your wall.

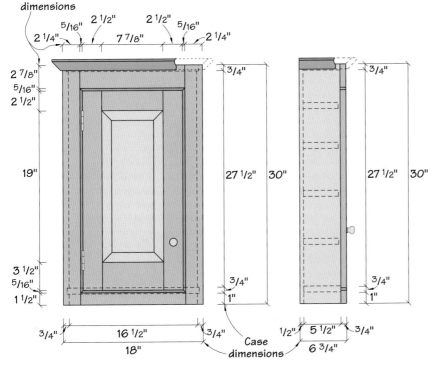

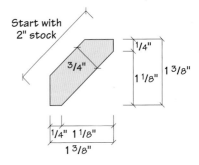

Here you can see how the bottom of the case acts as a door stop. This is one of the reasons I build my face frames first: I can make sure my bottom will be in perfect position.

Fit the face frame on the case. The stiles should hang ¹/₁₆" over the edge of the case so you can rout (or plane) them flush later.